Dear Visitor

Welcome to 'Ire
your guide to m.
well-known tourist attractions.

It will take you the length and breadth of this beautiful island, from kissing the Blarney Stone in County Cork to tasting a 'wee nip' of Old Bushmills Whiskey in County Antrim. Furthermore, you can relax in the knowledge that the more you see, the more you'll save.

In all, there are 108 attractions to choose from – a wide array of activities for all tastes and ages. 'Ireland at a Glimpse' enables you to enter a world of museums, castles, gardens, monuments and wildlife – every facet of Ireland's culture and heritage.

Children can see their favourite animals in zoos and wildlife parks, while adults can savour the magnificent surroundings of Gothic manors and historic homes.

Keep 'Ireland at a Glimpse' to hand, have an enjoyable stay, and be sure to visit the Emerald Isle again soon.

Peter Little

Peter Little
Chief Executive

TERMES ET CONDITIONS

1. Il est recommandé de bien lire les coupons avant de les utiliser. Les tarifs préférentiels ne s'appliquent qu'aux attractions et aux termes spécifiés.

2. Les coupons doivent être remis à l'entrée des attractions, en même temps que le paiement des droits d'entrée appropriés.

3. Les coupons ne sont pas valables après la date d'expiration indiquée.

4. Il est interdit d'utiliser ces coupons conjointement avec d'autres réductions ou promotions offertes en même temps par un centre d'attractions quelconque.

5. Les coupons ne sont pas remboursables en espèces.

6. La responsabilité de "Peter Little Publications" ou de ses représentants ne saurait être engagée en cas de rupture de contrat de la part d'un centre d'attractions quelconque ou de litige entre un centre d'attractions quelconque et un client quelconque. Cependant, "Peter Little Publications" s'efforcera d'assurer la conformité.

7. Les informations contenues dans ce guide ont été fournies par un tiers. Toute erreur ou omission concernant ces renseignements ne saurait engager la responsabilité de "Peter Little Publications".

8. Les clients visitent les endroits décrits dans ce guide entièrement à leurs risques et périls.

Cher visiteur,

Bienvenue à "Clin d'oeil sur l'Irlande", votre guide pratique sur tout un éventail des plus grandes attractions touristiques d'Irlande.

"Clin d'oeil sur l'Irlande" vous fera découvrir le charme et la beauté de tous les coins de cette île magnifique, depuis le Comté de Cork où vous pourrez embrasser la pierre de Blarney, jusqu'au Comté d'Antrim où l'ancienne distillerie de Bushmills vous offrira un petit verre de son fameux whiskey irlandais. En outre, vous pourrez vous détendre en sachant que plus vous visitez d'endroits, plus les économies que vous faites se multiplient.

En tout, plus de 100 attractions vous sont proposées - une myriade de loisirs qui conviennent à tous les goûts et à tous les âges.

"Clin d'oeil sur l'Irlande" vous permet de découvrir le monde des musées, des châteaux, des jardins, des monuments, de la faune et de la flore - toutes les facettes de la culture et du patrimoine irlandais.

Les enfants découvriront leurs animaux préférés en visitant les nombreux jardins zoologiques et parcs naturels, tandis que les adultes seront séduits par la splendeur des manoirs gothiques et des monuments historiques.

Gardez votre guide "Clin d'oeil sur l'Irlande" à portée de la main; nous espérons que votre séjour dans l'Ile d'Emeraude vous séduira et vous donnera l'envie de revenir très bientôt!

Peter Little

Peter Little
Directeur Général

GESCHÄFTSBEDINGUNGEN

1. Lesen Sie jeden Gutschein sorgfältig bevor Sie ihn benutzen. Ermäßigungen gibt es nur zu den genannten Veranstaltungen und zu den genannten Bedingungen.

2. Gutscheine müssen zusammen mit dem Eintrittsgeld bei Eintritt vorgelegt werden.

3. Gutscheine werden nach dem aufgedruckten Datum ungültig.

4. Gutscheine können nicht benutzt werden für Ermäßigungen anderer Veranstaltungen zur gleichen Zeit.

5. Gutscheine können nicht gegen Bargeld eingetauscht werden.

6. 'Peter Little Publications' oder seine Vertreter sind nicht verantwortlich wenn ein Veranstalter seinen Vertrag nicht einhält oder für Auseinandersetzungen zwischen Veranstaltern und Kunden. 'Peter Little Publications' wird jedoch versuchen eine Einigung herbeizuführen.

7. 'Peter Little Publications' übernimmt keine Verantwortung für fehlenden Text oder Druckfehler in dieser Broschüre, welche von einer anderen Firma erstellt wurde.

8. Der Besuch der in diesem Buch genannten Sehenswürdigkeiten geschieht auf eigenes Risiko.

Liebe(r) Reisende(r),

Willkommen zu 'Irland auf einen Blick', Ihrem Reiseführer zu vielen bekannten Sehenswürdigkeiten Irlands.

'Irland auf einen Blick' wird Sie kreuz und quer über diese wunderschöne Insel führen, beginnend mit dem 'Blarney Stein' in der Grafschaft Cork, den Sie mit den Lippen berühren sollen, bis hin zu der Grafschaft Antrim, zum Probieren des alten Bushmills' Whiskey. Überdies können Sie sich entspannen in dem Wissen, daß Sie, je mehr Sie besichtigen, je mehr können Sie sparen.

Insgesamt gibt es über 100 Attraktivitäten zur Auswahl - eine stattliche Reihe von Unternehmungen für jeden Geschmack und jedes Alter.

Mit 'Irland auf einen Blick' lernen Sie Museen, Schlösser, Gärten, Denkmäler und die Natur kennen, jede Facette von Irland's Kultur und Erbgut.

Kinder können ihre Lieblingstiere in Zoo's und Wildparks betrachten, während die Erwachsenen die prachtvolle Umgebung gothischer Herrensitze und geschichtlich bedeutender Wohnorte genießen können.

Halten Sie "Irland auf einen Blick' bereit, genießen Sie Ihren Aufenthalt dann werden Sie bestimmt die 'Grüne Insel' bald wieder besuchen.

Peter Little

Peter Little
Geschäftsführer

Table of Attractions

Voucher Number	Name of Attraction	County
1	Blarney Castle	Cork
2	Cobh, The Queenstown Story	Cork
3	Fota Wildlife Park	Cork
4	Jameson Heritage Centre	Cork
5	Cork City Gaol	Cork
6	Desmond Castle	Cork
7	Skellig Experience	Kerry
8	Kenmare Heritage Centre	Kerry
9	The Blasket Centre	Kerry
10	Blennerville Windmill	Kerry
11	Tralee & Dingle Railway	Kerry
12	Kerry the Kingdom	Kerry
13	Glin Castle	Limerick
14	Adare Heritage Centre	Limerick
15	Foynes Flying Boat Museum	Limerick
16	Celtic Park & Gardens	Limerick
17	Aillwee Cave	Clare
18	Craggaunowen	Clare
19	Ennis Friary	Clare
20	Lismore Heritage Centre	Waterford
21	Touraneena Heritage Centre	Waterford
22	Cashel Folk Village	Tipperary
23	Cahir Castle	Tipperary
24	Roscrea Castle and Damer House	Tipperary
25	Rothe House	Kilkenny
26	CityScope Exhibition	Kilkenny
27	Irish National Heritage Park	Wexford
28	West Gate Heritage Centre	Wexford
29	Russborough House	Wicklow
30	Powerscourt Gardens	Wicklow
31	Irish National Stud/ Japanese Gardens	Kildare

Table of Attractions

Voucher Number	Name of Attraction	County
● 32	Birr Castle Demesne	Offaly
● 33	Dvblinia	Dublin
● 34	National Wax Museum	Dublin
● 35	Dublin Zoo	Dublin
● 36	Phoenix Park Visitor Centre	Dublin
● 37	Irish Whiskey Corner	Dublin
● 38	Dublin Experience	Dublin
● 39	Dublin Castle	Dublin
● 40	Waterways Visitor Centre	Dublin
● 41	Butterstream Gardens	Meath
● 42	Athlone Castle Visitor Centre	Westmeath
● 43	Locke's Distillery Museum	Westmeath
● 44	Carrigglas Manor	Longford
● 45	Corlea Trackway Visitor Centre	Longford
● 46	Killykeen Forest Park	Cavan
● 47	Carraig Craft Visitors' Centre	Cavan
● 48	St Kilian's Heritage Centre	Cavan
● 49	Lough Rynn Estate	Leitrim
● 50	Patrick Kavanagh Centre	Monaghan
● 51	Ulster Canal Stores	Monaghan
● 52	Galway Irish Crystal Heritage Centre	Galway
● 53	Kylemore Abbey	Galway
● 54	Leenane Culture Centre	Galway
● 55	Coole	Galway
● 56	Foxford Woollen Mills	Mayo
● 57	Westport House	Mayo
● 58	Strokestown Park House, Museum & Gardens	Roscommon
● 59	King House	Roscommon
● 60	Animal Farm Visitor Centre	Roscommon
● 61	Lissadell House	Sligo

Table of Attractions

Voucher Number	Name of Attraction	County
● 62	Ionad Cois Locha	Donegal
● 63	Cavanacor House	Donegal
● 64	Lifford Old Courthouse	Donegal
● 65	Marble Arch Caves	Fermangh
● 66	Belleek Pottery	Fermangh
● 67	Florence Court	Fermangh
● 68	Castle Coole	Fermangh
● 69	Enniskillen Castle	Fermangh
● 70	Ulster American Folk Park	Tyrone
● 71	Ulster History Park	Tyrone
● 72	Tyrone Crystal	Tyrone
● 73	Wellbrook Beetling Mill	Tyrone
● 74	The Argory	Tyrone
● 75	Gray's Printing Press	Tyrone
● 76	An Creggan	Tyrone
● 77	Tower Museum	Derry
● 78	Springhill	Derry
● 79	Hezlett House	Derry
● 80	Old Bushmills Distillery	Antrim
● 81	Dunluce Centre	Antrim
● 82	Dunluce Castle	Antrim
● 83	Giant's Causeway	Antrim
● 84	Arthur Cottage	Antrim
● 85	Carrickfergus Castle	Antrim
● 86	Knightride Heritage Plaza	Antrim
● 87	Andrew Jackson/US Ranger	Antrim
● 88	Patterson's Spade Mill	Antrim
● 89	Irish Linen Centre	Antrim
● 90	Lagan Lookout	Belfast
● 91	Belfast Zoo	Belfast
● 92	Citybus Tour	Belfast
● 93	The Bronte Homeland	Down

Table of Attractions

Voucher Number	Name of Attraction	County
● 94	Ulster Folk & Transport Museum	Down
● 95	Mount Stewart	Down
● 96	Somme Heritage Centre	Down
● 97	Castle Espie- Wildfowl & Wetlands Trust	Down
● 98	Grey Abbey	Down
● 99	Exploris	Down
● 100	Streamvale Farm	Down
● 101	Rowallane	Down
● 102	Castleward	Down
● 103	The Navan Centre	Armagh
● 104	St Patrick's Trian	Armagh
● 105	Palace Stables	Armagh
● 106	Ardress House	Armagh
● 107	Lough Neagh Discovery Centre	Armagh
● 108	County Museum	Louth

Useful information for disabled or less abled visitors

The majority of the attractions featured in this guide are able to accommodate the disabled or less abled visitor and have provided facilities to make your visit an enjoyable one. In some attractions however access may be limited, for example, to the ground floor. In a small number of cases it would be unsuitable to visit.

We would recommend that you contact the attraction before your visit to find out exactly what facilities are available. The telephone number appears on the front of each voucher.

A sample of just 3 of the new attractions featured

Dublin Castle

Galway Irish Crystal Heritage Centre

King House

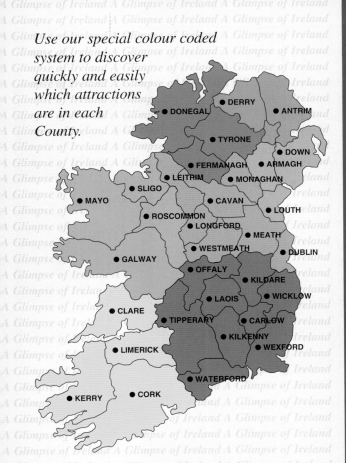

Use our special colour coded system to discover quickly and easily which attractions are in each County.

- DERRY
- DONEGAL
- ANTRIM
- TYRONE
- DOWN
- FERMANAGH
- ARMAGH
- LEITRIM
- MONAGHAN
- SLIGO
- MAYO
- CAVAN
- ROSCOMMON
- LOUTH
- LONGFORD
- MEATH
- WESTMEATH
- GALWAY
- DUBLIN
- OFFALY
- KILDARE
- LAOIS
- WICKLOW
- CLARE
- TIPPERARY
- CARLOW
- KILKENNY
- LIMERICK
- WEXFORD
- WATERFORD
- KERRY
- CORK

As you can see, we've given each region a different colour. Simply refer to our Table of Attractions and you'll see that every voucher has a specific colour code – this corresponds with one of the 7 areas on the map.

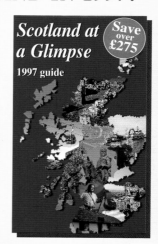

Blarney Castle (1)

**Blarney
Co Cork**

Tel: (021) 385252

Present this voucher and we
will allow you one free
admission to the Castle when
a second of equal or greater
value is purchased.

Blarney Castle Estate

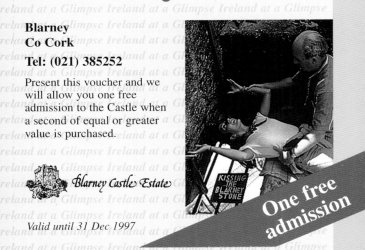

**One free
admission**

Valid until 31 Dec 1997

Cobh, (2)
The Queenstown Story

**Cobh Railway Station
Cobh, Co Cork**

Tel: (021) 813591

Present this voucher and
receive one free admission
when a second of equal or
greater value is purchased.

*Cobh
The*
Queenstown
Story

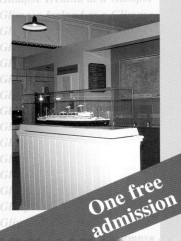

**One free
admission**

Valid until 31 Dec 1997

Blarney Castle

Blarney Castle is one of Ireland's oldest and most historic castles. It was an ancient stronghold of the MacCarthys, Lords of Muskerry, and is one of the strongest fortresses in Munster. Its walls are 18 feet thick in places. The famous Blarney Stone is embedded in the Battlements.

Opening times:

Mon – Sat:	May	9am - 6.30pm.
	June-July-August	9am - 7pm.
	September	9am - 6.30pm.
	October–April	9am - sundown (or 6pm)
Sundays:	Summer	9.30am - 5.30pm.
	Winter	9.30am - sundown.

Potential saving - £3.00.

Based on 1996 adult admission price. (Note: 1997 savings may be even greater as many 1997 prices were not available at time of printing.)

Cobh, The Queenstown Story

From 1848 to 1950, over six million adults and children emigrated from Ireland. About 2.5 million left Cobh, making it the single most important port of emigration. Now Cobh's unique origins, its history and legacy are dramatically recalled at The Queenstown Story – a multi-media exhibition at Cobh's Victorian Railway Station.

● Explore the conditions on board the early emigrant vessels, including the dreaded 'coffin ship'.

● Learn about an 'Irish Wake', the special farewell for emigrating sons and daughters, many of whom never returned to Ireland.

● Experience life aboard a convict ship leaving Cove for Australia in 1801.

Opening times:

January – December   Daily   10am to 6pm.
(Last admission 5pm.)

Potential saving - £3.50.

Based on 1996 adult admission price. (Note: 1997 savings may be even greater as many 1997 prices were not available at time of printing.)

Fota Wildlife Park

**Carrigtwohill
Co Cork**

Tel: (021) 812678

Present this voucher and receive one free admission for a child when accompanied by two full-paying adults.

One free child admission

Valid until 31 Dec 1997

Jameson Heritage Centre

**Midleton
Co Cork**

Tel: (021) 613594/6

Present this voucher and receive one free admission when a second of equal or greater value is purchased.

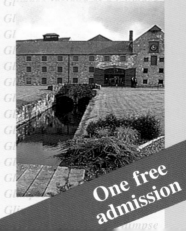

One free admission

Valid until 31 Dec 1997

Fota Wildlife Park

Fota Wildlife Park has over 70 species of exotic wildlife in open natural surroundings with no obvious barriers. Giraffes, zebra and ostrich enjoy 40 acres of grassland, monkeys swing through trees on islands, while wallabies, macaws and lemurs have complete freedom of the Park. Only the cheetahs have a conventional fence. Ten miles from Cork city (turn for Cobh from N.25).

Opening times:

April – October. Phone (021) 812678 for more details.

Potential saving - £2.00.

Based on 1996 child admission price. (Note: 1997 savings may be even greater as many 1997 prices were not available at time of printing.)

Jameson Heritage Centre

A tour of the Jameson Heritage Centre is a journey through the story of Irish Whiskey by means of an audio-visual presentation. Follow the old Distillery Trail through mills, maltings and kilns. View the largest pot still in the world and sample the internationally renowned Jameson Whiskey in the bar before relaxing in the Gallery Restaurant.

Opening times:

March – October; 7 days; tours – 10am - 6pm.

Last tour commences at 4pm.

Potential saving - £3.50.

Based on 1996 adult admission price. (Note: 1997 savings may be even greater as many 1997 prices were not available at time of printing.)

Cork City Gaol ⁵

Sunday's Well
Cork
Co Cork

Tel: (021) 305022

Present this voucher and
receive one free admission
when a second of equal or
greater value is purchased.

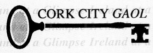

CORK CITY *GAOL*

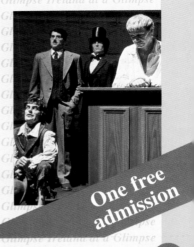

Valid until 31 Dec 1997

One free admission

Desmond Castle ⁶

Kinsale
Co Cork
Tel: (021) 774855

Present this voucher and
receive one free admission
when a second of equal or
greater value is purchased.

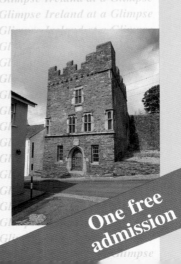

Valid until 31 Dec 1996

One free admission

Cork City Gaol

Situated 2Km from Cork's main street is Cork City Gaol Heritage Centre at Sunday's Well. Despite its majestic appearance, this prison building housed 19th Century prisoners, often in wretched conditions. Furnished cells, amazingly lifelike characters, sound effects and fascinating exhibitions allow the visitor to experience day to day life for prisoners and gaoler. A spectacular Audio Visual tells the social history and contrasting lifestyles of the period 1824-1923, and why some people turned to crime.

There are English, French, German, Italian, Irish & Spanish tours available. Other facilities include Coffee and Souvenir Shops, parking, wheelchair access.

Opening times:

March - October	Daily	9.30am - 6pm.
November - Febuary	Daily tours	10.30am and 2.30pm.
	Weekends	10am - 5pm.

Potential saving - £3.00.

Based on 1996 adult admission price. (Note: 1997 savings may be even greater as many 1997 prices were not available at time of printing.)

Desmond Castle

Built as a custom house by the Earl of Desmond c. A.D. 1500, Desmond Castle has had a colourful history, ranging from Spanish occupation in 1601 to use as a prison for captured American sailors during the American War of Independence. Known locally as 'The French Prison' after a tragic fire in which 54 prisoners, mainly French seamen, died in 1747. The castle was also used as a borough jail from 1791 to the onset of the Great Famine when it was used as an auxiliary workhouse tending to the starving populace.

Opening times:

Mid April - Mid June	Tuesday - Sunday	10am - 1pm & 2pm - 5pm.
(Closed Mondays except Bank Holidays.)		
Mid June - Mid Sept	Daily	9am - 6pm.
Mid Sept - Early Oct	Monday - Saturday	9am - 5pm.
	Sunday	10am - 5pm.

Potential saving - £1.00.

Based on 1996 adult admission price. (Note: 1997 savings may be even greater as many 1997 prices were not available at time of printing.)

The Skellig Experience

Valentia Island
Ring of Kerry
Co Kerry

Tel: (066) 76306

Present this voucher and receive one free admission when a second of equal or greater value is purchased.

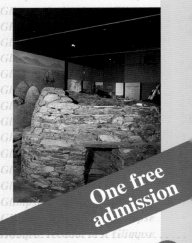

One free admission

Valid until 31 Dec 1997

The Kenmare Heritage Centre

The Square
Kenmare
Co Kerry

Tel: (064) 41233

Present this voucher and receive one free admission when a second of equal or greater value is purchased.

One free admission

Valid until 31 Dec 1997

The Skellig Experience

'The Skellig Experience' is an exciting visitor Centre which opened in April 1992 on Valentia Island. It is located directly opposite the attractive fishing village of Portmagee. The Centre interprets in a lively and non academic way the following themes.

The life and work of the early Christian Irish Monks on Skellig Michael. The history of the Light Houses and Light Keepers of Skellig Michael from 1820 to 1987. The sea birds of Little Skellig and Skellig Michael. The underwater sea life of Skelligs.

A 16 minute Audio Visual programme 'The Call of The Skelligs' brings the visitor on a personal guided tour of the monastery on Skellig Michael. Sound tours in 6 languages are also available.

Opening times:
Mid April to end September: Daily   10am - 7pm.

Potential saving - £3.00.

Based on 1996 adult admission price. (Note: 1997 savings may be even greater as many 1997 prices were not available at time of printing.)

The Kenmare Heritage Centre

The Kenmare Heritage Centre is located in a beautifully restored old building in the centre of Kenmare. The entrance is through the Tourist Information Office.

The Centre cover themes such as:

Kenmare Lace.
Famous visitors to Kenmare.
The Nun of Kenmare.
The history of Kenmare.
Historical sites in Kenmare.
The effects of the Famine in Kenmare.
The Landlords of Kenmare.
Personal sound tours available (English, French, German).

Opening times:
May - September   Monday - Saturday   9.30am - 5.30pm.
                  Sunday   11am - 1pm
                                      & 2.15pm - 5pm.

Potential saving - £2.00.

Based on 1996 adult admission price. (Note: 1997 savings may be even greater as many 1997 prices were not available at time of printing.)

Ionad an Bhlascaoid Mhóir

(The Blasket Centre)
Dún Chaoin
Trá Lí, Co Chiarraí
Tel: (066) 56444

Present this voucher and
receive one free admission
when a second of equal or
greater value is purchased.

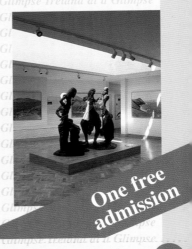

One free admission

Valid until 31 Dec 1997

Blennerville Windmill Visitor and Craft Centre

Blennerville
Tralee, Co Kerry
Tel: (066) 21064

Cordially invite you and your
guest to enjoy one
complimentary admission
when a second
of equal or
greater value
is purchased.

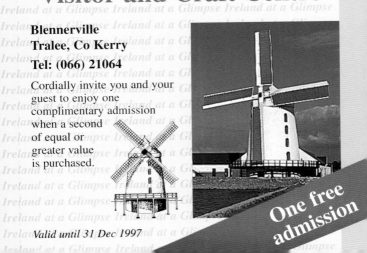

One free admission

Valid until 31 Dec 1997

Ionad an Bhlascaoid Mhóir

The Great Blasket Island off the Dingle coast is renowned for its historic, cultural and literary heritage. In this context, it has been designated a National Historic Park. The Blasket Centre, on the mainland at Dún Chaoin, celebrates the Irish Language, the distinctive character of the Islanders and the unique achievements of the Island writers.

Opening times:

Easter - June	Daily	10am - 6pm.
July - August	Daily	10am - 7pm.
September	Daily	10am - 6pm.

Last admission 45 minutes before closing.
(Open for bookings during the winter.)

Opening times may change, check with site beforehand.

Potential saving - £2.50.

Based on 1996 adult admission price. (Note: 1997 savings may be even greater as many 1997 prices were not available at time of printing.)

Blennerville Windmill Visitor and Craft Centre

Blennerville Windmill is the focal point of a major visitor centre and craft complex on the shores of Tralee Bay. The visitor centre comprises the working Windmill, audio-visual presentation, exhibition gallery, craft workshops, craft shop and restaurant. Visitors receive a guided tour of the five-story windmill and can view the various stages of the grain milling process.

Opening times:

March – October	Daily	10am - 6pm.

Potential saving - £2.75.

Based on 1996 adult admission price. (Note: 1997 savings may be even greater as many 1997 prices were not available at time of printing.)

Tralee & Dingle Steam Railway

Ballyard
Tralee, Co Kerry

Tel: (066) 21064

Cordially invite you and your
guest to enjoy one
complimentary admission
when a second of equal or
greater value is purchased.

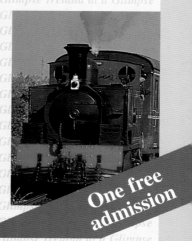

One free admission

Valid until 31 Dec 1997

Kerry the Kingdom

Ashe Memorial Hall
Tralee
Co Kerry

Tel: (066) 27777

Present this voucher and
receive one free child
admission when accompanied
by a full-paying adult.

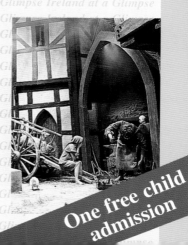

One free child admission

Valid until 31 Dec 1997

Tralee & Dingle Steam Railway

Experience the fascination of steam travel on Europe's most westerly railway. The Tralee & Dingle Steam Railway (1891 – 1953) was one of the world's most famous narrow-gauge lines. Now the Tralee-Blennerville section of the historic railway has been restored and steam trains operate hourly for Ballyard Station (near Aqua Dome) to Blennerville Windmill Complex (3km). The railway is featured in the TV series "Great Railway Journeys of the World".

Opening times:

Steam Trains operate daily from April to September, 11am-5pm, (except 2nd Sunday/Monday of May, June, July, August and September).

Potential saving - £2.75.

Based on 1996 adult admission price. (Note: 1997 savings may be even greater as many 1997 prices were not available at time of printing.)

Kerry the Kingdom

Kerry the Kingdom incorporates three superb attractions:

Kerry in Colour:
A multi-image audio-visual presentation on Kerry's spectacular scenery.

Kerry County Museum:
Traces man's history in Kerry from 5,000 B.C.

Geraldine Tralee:
Travel by time car through the reconstructed streets, houses and Abbey of Geraldine Tralee – seat of power of the Anglo Norman Fitzgeralds during the Middle Ages.

Opening times:

March – October	10am - 6pm.
August	10am - 7pm.
November – December	2pm - 5pm.

Potential saving - £2.50.

Based on 1996 child admission price. (Note: 1997 savings may be even greater as many 1997 prices were not available at time of printing.)

Glin Castle

Glin
Co Limerick
Tel: (068) 34112

Present this voucher and
receive one free admission
when a second of equal or
greater value is purchased.

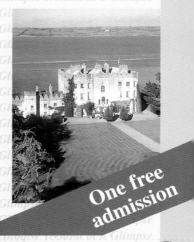

One free admission

Valid until 31 Dec 1997

Adare Heritage Centre

Main Street
Adare
Co Limerick
Tel: (061) 396666

Present this voucher and
receive one free admission
when a second of equal or
greater value is purchased.

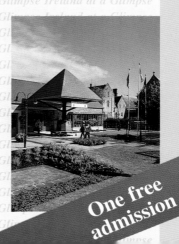

One free admission

Valid until 31 Dec 1997

Glin Castle

Glin Castle, home of 29th Knight of Glin, has been in the FitzGerald family for 700 years. Neoclassical hall, elaborate plasterwork, flying staircase and mahogany library with hidden door all surveyed by ancestral portraits. Pleasure park, walled kitchen garden and spectacular spring garden with rare plant species. Castle guarded by three toy fort lodges, one of which is a craft shop and tearooms.

Opening times:

May - June: Open daily   10am - 12 noon
                                                   2pm - 4pm.

(Guided tours on the half hour.)

Potential saving - £3.00.

Based on 1996 adult admission price. (Note: 1997 savings may be even greater as many 1997 prices were not available at time of printing.)

Adare Heritage Centre

Situated in Ireland's most picturesque village, the Adare Heritage Centre allows you to experience this area's unique history, spanning the years from 1233 to the present day. The story is told through realistic model enactments and audio visuals in French, Italian, German, Irish and English. Also included in the Centre is a Tourist Information Office, quality craft shop, a splendid restaurant and a public library. Free coach and car parking available.

Opening times:

March - May	Daily	10am - 5pm.
June - September	Daily	8.30am - 6.30pm.
October - November	Daily	10am - 5pm.

Potential saving - £2.00.

Based on 1996 adult admission price. (Note: 1997 savings may be even greater as many 1997 prices were not available at time of printing.)

The Foynes Flying Boat Museum 15

Foynes
Co Limerick
Tel: (069) 65416

Present this voucher and
receive one free admission
when a second of equal or
greater value is purchased.

THE FOYNES
FLYING BOAT
MUSEUM

Valid until 31 Dec 1997

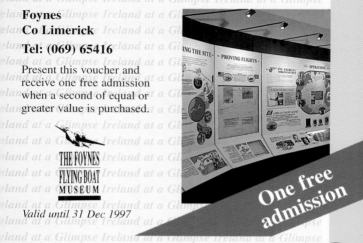

One free
admission

Celtic Park & Gardens 16

Kilcornan (N69)
Co Limerick
Tel: (061) 394243

Present this voucher and
receive one free admission
when a second of equal or
greater value is purchased.

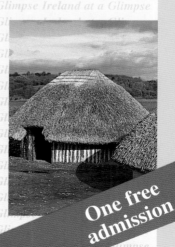

One free
admission

Valid until 31 Dec 1997

The Foynes Flying Boat Museum

During the 1930's and early 1940's, the port of Foynes was the fulcrum point for all air traffic between the United States and Europe.

The famous Flying Boats of BOAC, Pan Am, American Export Airlines were frequent visitors, carrying a diverse range of people, from celebrities to refugees.

The Museum recalls this era with a comprehensive range of exhibits, graphic illustrations and a 1940's style cinema.

It was here in Foynes in 1942 during the flying boat days that Chef Joe Sheirdan invented the world famous drink IRISH COFFEE and this story is illustrated also in the Museum.

Opening times:

March 31 - October 31	Daily	10am - 6pm.
Last admission		5.30 pm.

Potential saving - £3.00.

based on 1996 Adult admission price. (Note: 1997 savings may be even greater as many 1997 prices were not available at time of printing.)

Celtic Park & Gardens

Where Celtic Life is a Reality

Situated for over 2000 years on 30 acres of unspoilt territory. First owned by the ancient Celtic Family of O'Donovan, also by the Norman Fitzgeralds and latterly by Cromwell's General, Sir Hardress Waller's Family up to the 1930's.

On Display are a Stone Circle, Mass Rock, Dolmen, Wood Church, Lime Kiln, Royal Chair, Lake Dwelling, Ogham Stone, Cooking Site, Stone Church, Holy Well and a Ring Fort.

The Classic Gardens are an oasis of quiet and beauty. 1000 Roses, Shrubs, Rockery, Herbaceous Beds, Lily Pond, Colonnades and Gravel Paths are enjoyed by all who visit.

16 Km from Limerick City on N69 to Tralee, 8Km from Adare Village, adjacent to Curragh Chase Forest Park.

Opening times:

Mid March - 31 October	Daily	9am - 7pm

Potential saving - £3.00.

based on 1996 Adult admission price. (Note: 1997 savings may be even greater as many 1997 prices were not available at time of printing.)

Aillwee Cave

Ballyvaughan
Co Clare

Tel: (065) 77036

Cordially invite you to one free admission when a second of equal or greater value is purchased.

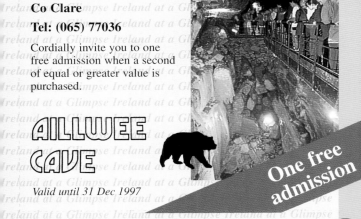

AILLWEE CAVE

Valid until 31 Dec 1997

One free admission

Craggaunowen

Kilmurry
Sixmilebridge
Co Clare

Tel: (061) 367178

Cordially invites you and your guest to enjoy one complimentary ADMISSION when a second ADMISSION of equal or greater value is purchased.

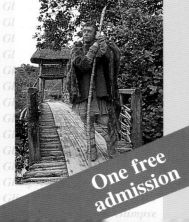

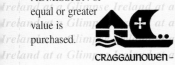

CRAGGAUNOWEN –
The Living Past

Valid until 31 Dec 1997

One free admission

Aillwee Cave

Aillwee Cave, IRELAND'S PREMIER SHOWCAVE.
Guided tours every ten minutes showing spectacular caverns
and unique bear pits. The award-winning building houses a
cafe and a distinctly different craft shop.

Opening times:

OPEN DAILY from 10am, mid March to early November.

Last tour: 6.30pm July and August.
               5.30pm other months.

Potential saving - £3.95.

Based on 1996 adult admission price. (Note: 1997 savings may be even
greater as many 1997 prices were not available at time of printing.)

Craggaunowen

Where Celtic Life is brought to life', is situated in the
wooded farmland of Co Clare. Consisting of reconstructions
of prehistoric and early historic farmsteads (located in the
grounds of a medieval Irish Chieftain's Castle), guides – in
costume and in character – tell of life in the past. Ancient
breeds of animals, including Bronze Age Sheep and Iron
Age Wild Boar, add enormously to the visitor's enjoyment.
The colour picture on the front of the voucher features
'Caomhan The Celt', a major participant in our 'Living Past
Experience'.

Opening times:

Mid March - Late October   Daily   10am - 6pm.

Potential saving - £3.80.

Based on 1996 adult admission price. (Note: 1997 savings may be even
greater as many 1997 prices were not available at time of printing.)

Ennis Friary

Ennis
Co Clare

Tel: (065) 29100

Present this voucher and
receive one free admission
when a second of equal or
greater value is purchased.

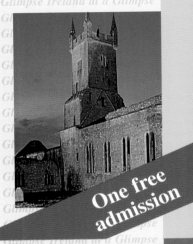

Valid until 31 Dec 1997

One free admission

Lismore Heritage Centre

The Courthouse
Lismore
Co Waterford

Tel: (058) 54975

Present this voucher and
receive one free admission
when a second of equal or
greater value is purchased.

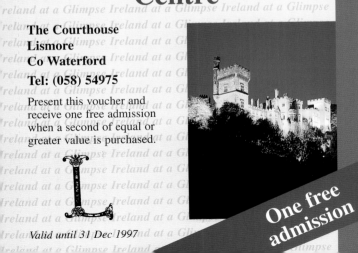

Valid until 31 Dec 1997

One free admission

Ennis Friary

A 13th Century Franciscan Friary founded by the O'Briens, Kings of Thomond. The well-preserved ruins have a splendid splayed, pointed five light east window, while some fine specimens of gothic windows adorn the south transept. The most outstanding features are a series of 15/16th Century sculptures carved in the local hard limestone. The McMahon tomb is probably the most renowned example with its five panels depicting the passion.

Opening times:

Late May – late Sept   Daily   9.30am - 6.30pm.

Last admission 45 minutes before closing.

Opening times may change, check with site beforehand.

Potential saving - £1.00.

Based on 1996 adult admission price. (Note: 1997 savings may be even greater as many 1997 prices were not available at time of printing.)

Lismore Heritage Centre

The old Courthouse has now become Lismore Heritage Centre where you can experience the rich history of the town and its surroundings. Here you can view the Lismore Experience and the award-winning multi-media presentation in which your host Dr Declan (alias Niall Toibin) takes you on an enthralling journey through time, starting with the arrival of St Carthage in 636, and bringing you up to the present.

Opening times:

April/May:	Mon – Friday	10.00am - 6.00pm.
	Sunday	12 noon - 6.00pm.
June/July/August:	Monday – Saturday	9.30am - 6.00pm.
	Sunday	12 noon - 6.00pm.
September:	Mon – Saturday	10.00am - 6.00pm.
	Sunday	12 noon - 6.00pm.
October:	Sunday	2.00pm - 5.30pm.

Potential saving - £2.50.

Based on 1996 adult admission price. (Note: 1997 savings may be even greater as many 1997 prices were not available at time of printing.)

Touraneena Heritage Centre

Touraneena
Ballinamult
Co Waterford

Tel: (058) 47353

Present this voucher and receive one free admission when a second of equal or greater value is purchased.

Valid until 31 Dec 1997

One free admission

Cashel Folk Village

Dominic Street
Cashel
Co Tipperary
Tel: (062) 62525

Cordially invite you to one free admission when a second of equal or greater value is purchased.

Cashel Folk Village

Valid until 31 Dec 1997

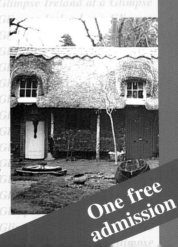

One free admission

Touraneena Heritage Centre

On the R672 between Dungarvan and Clonmel, Touraneena Heritage Centre is sited on the 300 year old thatched farmhouse, home of the O'Keefe family for the past eight generations. Depicting Irish Rural life in 1890s, the staff are dressed in costume. Hands on demonstrations, bread and scone baking over a turf fire using original crane and oven pots in farmhouse kitchen and butter making in the dairy. Featuring Blacksmiths forge, gypsy wagon, stable boys loft, incubator and vintage farm machinery.

Facilities include picnic tables, tearoom, adventure playground, pet farm, pony and tractor rides, gift shop, large car park and toilet block. Irish Dancing Sundays July/August pm.

Opening times:

April-October   7 days   10am to 6pm.

Potential saving - £3.00.

Based on 1996 adult admission price. (Note: 1997 savings may be even greater as many 1997 prices were not available at time of printing.)

Cashel Folk Village

Visit the thatched 18th, 19th and 20th Century 'Village', consisting of Tinker's Caravan, well, kitchen, pub, butcher's shop, forge, tool and trades display, exhibition hall, Penal Chapel and museum.

Themes: Penal Times, The Great Famine, 1916 Rising and The War of Independence.

Opening times:

March – October   7 days   10am - 7.30pm.

Potential saving - £2.00.

Based on 1996 adult admission price. (Note: 1997 savings may be even greater as many 1997 prices were not available at time of printing.)

Cahir Castle

23

Cahir
Co Tipperary
Tel: (052) 41011

Present this voucher and
receive one free admission
when a second of equal or
greater value is purchased.

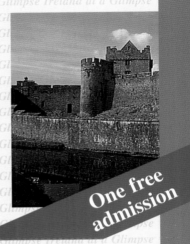

Valid until 31 Dec 1997

One free admission

Roscrea Castle and Damer House

24

Roscrea
Co Tipperary
Tel: (0505) 21850

Present this voucher and
receive one free admission
when a second of equal or
greater value is purchased.

Valid until 31 Dec 1997

One free admission

Cahir Castle

Cahir Castle is one of Ireland's largest and best preserved castles, situated on a rocky island on the River Suir. The castle's attractions include an excellent audio-visual show called "Partly Hidden and Partly Revealed" (English/French/German/Italian). The show informs visitors of all the main sites of the area. There are also several exhibitions.

Opening times:

April – mid June	Daily	10am - 6pm.
Mid June – mid Sept	Daily	9am - 7.30pm.
Mid Sept – mid Oct	Daily	10am - 6pm.
Mid Oct – March	Daily	10am - 1pm & 2pm - 4.30pm.

Last admission 45 minutes before closing.

Opening times may change, check with site beforehand.

Potential saving - £2.00.

Based on 1996 adult admission price. (Note: 1997 savings may be even greater as many 1997 prices were not available at time of printing.)

Roscrea Castle and Damer House

The 13th century stone castle consists of a gate tower, curtain walls and two corner towers. In the castle courtyard stands the 18th century Queen Anne style Damer House. The site is managed in conjunction with the Roscrea Heritage Society.

Opening times:

June – September   Daily   9.30am - 6.00pm.
(Last admission 45 minutes before closing.)

Opening times may change, check with site beforehand.

Ring **0505 21850** for winter hours.

Potential saving - £2.50.

Based on 1996 adult admission price. (Note: 1997 savings may be even greater as many 1997 prices were not available at time of printing.)

Rothe House

Parliament Street
Kilkenny
Co Kilkenny
Tel: (056) 22893

Present this voucher and
receive one free admission
when a second of equal or
greater value
is purchased.

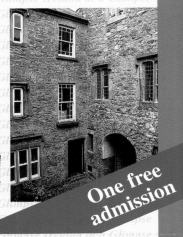

Rothe House, built 1594

Valid until 31 Dec 1997

One free admission

CityScope Exhibition

Shee Alms House
Rose Inn Street
Kilkenny
Co Kilkenny
Tel: (056) 51500

Present this voucher and
receive one free admission
when a second
of equal or
greater value
is purchased.

CITYSCOPE

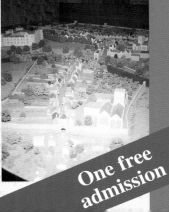

Valid until 31 Dec 1997

One free admission

Rothe House

Recently restored Tudor merchant house, Rothe House was built in 1594, by John Rothe for his wife, Rose Archer. It consists of three stone buildings divided by cobbled court yards. Museum exhibits, a period costume collection and a genealogical study centre are housed there. It is the headquarters of the Kilkenny Archaeological Society.

Received AIB 'Better Ireland' Award in 1995 and Gulbenkian Award for 'Best Improved Museum' in 1995.

Members of the IHP, IFHF and FLHS.

Opening times:

April - Oct	Monday - Saturday	10.30am - 5pm.
	Sunday	3pm - 5pm.
Nov - March	Monday - Saturday	1pm - 5pm.
	Sunday	3pm - 5pm.

Potential saving - £2.00.

Based on 1996 adult admission price. (Note: 1997 savings may be even greater as many 1997 prices were not available at time of printing.)

CityScope Exhibition

The CityScope exhibition is centred on an accurately reconstructed scale model of Kilkenny as it was in 1640. The walled city is depicted at the height of its power and influence and is used to tell the evolving story of the Medieval Capital and, in particular, to convey a sense of the every day life, work, and living pattern. A computer controlled battery of lights, using state of the art electronics makes the 22 minutes presentation one of the most exciting and imaginative portrayals of Ireland's colourful past – performances every half hour.

Opening times:

March - September	Daily	9am - 5pm.
October - November	Monday - Friday	9am - 5pm.

Potential saving - £1.00.

Based on 1996 adult admission price. (Note: 1997 savings may be even greater as many 1997 prices were not available at time of printing.)

Irish National Heritage Park

Ferrycarrig
Co Wexford

Tel: (053) 20733

Present this voucher and receive
one free admission when a second
of equal or greater value is
purchased.

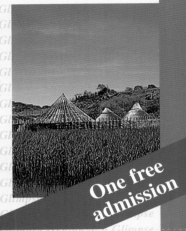

One free admission

Valid until 31 Dec 1997

West Gate Heritage Centre

Spawell Road
Wexford
Co Wexford

Tel: (053) 46506

Present this voucher and
receive one free admission
when a second of equal
or greater value
is purchased.

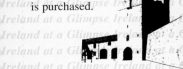

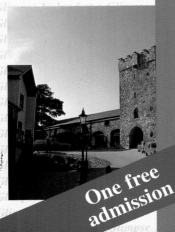

One free admission

Valid until 31 Dec 1997

Irish National Heritage Park

'Where Ireland's Heritage Trail Starts': Fourteen Historical Sites set in a magnificent 35-acre mature forest; explaining Ireland's history from the Stone and Bronze Age into the mighty Celtic period and concluding with the Viking and Norman influences. Sites included are the Mesolithic Camp, Portal Dolmen, Stone Circle, Ringfort, 10th Century Monastery, Crannog, Viking Boatyard (2 full-size ships), and Norman Motte and Bailey.

- Many hands-on demonstrations.
- Audio-visual, Guided Tours.
- Craft Shop, Coffee Shop and Picnic Tables.

Opening times:

From 17 March – early November.
Open 7 days a week: 10am to 7pm.

Please allow two hours for a visit.

Potential saving - £3.50.

Based on 1996 adult admission price. (Note: 1997 savings may be even greater as many 1997 prices were not available at time of printing.)

West Gate Heritage Centre

The West Gate Centre combines with the Ancient and historic Selskar Abbey to be the perfect setting to understand the Historical Development of Wexford. Situated in the heart of the Viking and Norman walled town, the Centre holds a 52 seat Audio-Visual Theatre which presents the colourful Cosmopolitan History of this Ancient town. In the Tower Gallery there are various ongoing Exhibitions.

Opening times:

May - October   Monday - Saturday   10.30am - 1pm.
                                        & 2pm - 5pm.

Opening hours may change, ring **(053) 23111** to confirm times

Potential saving - £1.50.

Based on 1996 adult admission price. (Note: 1997 savings may be even greater as many 1997 prices were not available at time of printing.)

Russborough House

Russborough
Blessington
Co Wicklow

Tel: (045) 865239

Cordially invite you to one
free admission when a second
of equal or greater value is
purchased.

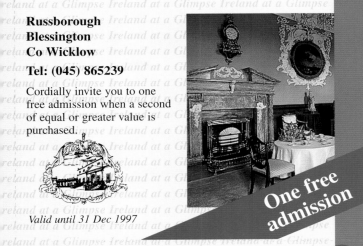

Valid until 31 Dec 1997

One free
admission

Powerscourt Gardens

Enniskerry
Co Wicklow

Tel: (01) 286 7676

Present this voucher and
receive one free admission
when a second of equal or
greater value is purchased.

POWERSCOURT
ESTATE

Valid until 31 Dec 1997

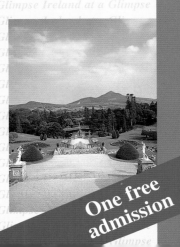

One free
admission

Russsborough House

Russsborough House is the finest house in Ireland open to the public. Built between 1740 and 1750 in the Palladian style by Richard Castle (Cassel) with fine stucco ceilings by the Francini brothers. Home of the internationally famous Beit Collection of paintings, it is beautifully maintained and lavishly furnished with fine displays of silver, bronzes, porcelain, fine furniture, tapestries and carpets.

Opening times:

Easter-May	Sundays & Bank Hols	10.30am - 5.30pm.
June-August	Daily	10.30am - 5.30pm.
September	Monday-Saturday	10.30am - 2.30pm.
	Sunday	10.30am - 5.30pm.
October	Sundays & Bank Hols	10.30am - 5.30pm.

Potential saving - £3.00.

Based on 1996 adult admission price to the main rooms. (Note: 1997 savings may be even greater as many 1997 prices were not available at time of printing.)

Powerscourt Gardens

One of the World's Great Gardens situated 12 miles south of Dublin in the foothills of the Wicklow Mountains. The word garden belies the magnitude of this creation which stretches out over 45 acres. A sublime blend of formal gardens, sweeping terraces, statuary and ornamental lakes together with secret hollows, rambling walks, walled gardens and over 200 variations of trees and shrubs. The gardens were begun by Sir Richard Windfield in the 1740's. Powerscourt House is currently under rennovation and is due to open to the public in the summer of 1997. Close by on the edge of the Estate is Ireland's Highest Waterfall which has been a favourite family picnic spot for years (separate admission). Facilities include tea rooms, craft shop, garden centre and children's play area.

Opening times:
Mid March - end of December   Daily   9.30 am - 5.30 pm. (including Sundays and Bank Holidays)

Potential saving - £3.00.

Based on 1996 adult admission price. (Note: 1997 savings may be even greater as many 1997 prices were not available at time of printing.)

The Irish National Stud/Japanese Gardens

Tully
Kildare Town
Co Kildare

Tel: (045) 522963

Present this voucher and receive one free admission. when a second of equal value is purchased.

Valid until 31 Dec 1997

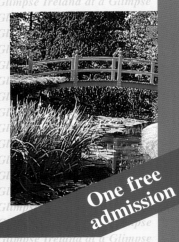

One free admission

Birr Castle Demesne

Rosse Row
Birr
Co Offaly

Tel: (0509) 20336

Cordially invite you to one free admission when a second of equal or greater value is purchased.

Valid until 31 Dec 1997

One free admission

The Irish National Stud/Japanese Gardens

The Irish National Stud and Japanese Gardens are situated at Tully, Kildare, just 30 miles south of Dublin. Visitors can enjoy seeing magnificent stallions, mares and foals, visiting the Horse Museum which includes a skeleton of the legendary Arkle, and taking a leisurely stroll through the sophisticated yet relaxing Japanese Gardens, which portray the story of 'The Life of Man'.

Opening times:

12 February to 12 November inclusive: 9.30am - 6pm.

Potential saving - £5.00.

Based on 1996 adult admission price. (Note: 1997 savings may be even greater as many 1997 prices were not available at time of printing.)

Birr Castle Demesne

Rated with five stars in the official list of Gardens of Outstanding Historic Interest in the Republic of Ireland, and doubled-starred in the Good Gardens Guide, the Birr Castle Demesne is over 50 ha in extent. One of Europe's finest ornamental gardens, with exotic blooms and shrubs. Features the world's tallest box hedges, lake, fernery, fountain, rivers and waterfalls, the Birr Castle Demesne is an earthly paradise.

The Great Rosse Telescope erected in 1845, is now fully rebuilt with viewing platform.

Facilities also include a Tourist Office and an excellent Coffee Shop serving lunch and tea.

Opening times:

January - March & November - December	9am - 1pm.
	2pm - 5pm.
April - October	9am - 6pm.

Open every day throughout the year.

Potential saving - £3.20.

Based on 1996 adult admission price. (Note: 1997 savings may be even greater as many 1997 prices were not available at time of printing.)

Dvblinia

St Michael's Hill
Christ Church
Dublin 8

Tel: (01) 6794611

Present this voucher and
receive one free admission
when a second of equal or
greater value is purchased.
(Note: Includes
admission to Christ
Church Cathedral.)

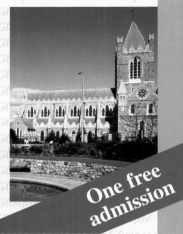

One free admission

Valid until 31 Dec 1997

National Wax Museum

Granby Row
Parnell Square
Dublin 1

Tel: (01) 8726340

Present this voucher and
receive one free admission
when a second of equal or
greater value is purchased.

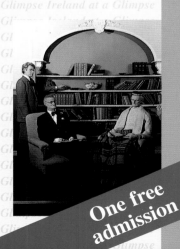

One free admission

Valid until 31 Dec 1997

Dvblinia

Dvblinia tells the story of medieval Dublin. The Journey Through Time introduces you to major events in Dublin's history; the scale model, with commentary and lighting, shows how the town looked 500 years ago; artefacts excavated at the famous Wood Quay site and life-size reconstructions of medieval scenes will fascinate you. Experience the harsh realities of the stocks and the pillory! How would you look in a suit of armour? Or dressed in the flowing robes of the middle ages? Use our 'photo-opportunity' board to see yourself as others might have seen you! Climb the 17th century tower for a panoramic view of modern Dublin and finish your visit by crossing the elegant bridge to Christ Church Cathedral.

Opening times:

October - March: Monday - Saturday   11am - 4pm.
                     Sunday/Bank Holiday   10am - 4.30pm.
April - September   Daily   10am - 5pm.

Potential saving - £3.95.

Based on 1996 adult admission price. (Note: 1997 savings may be even greater as many 1997 prices were not available at time of printing.)

National Wax Museum

Discover a world where fantasy and reality combine and heroes of the past and the present come alive before your eyes! See the Children's World of Fairytale and Fantasy. This display is truly a joy for children as they wander through the Kingdom of Fairytales.

The main section of the wax exhibition broadly reflects the historical and cultural development of Ireland.

The Chamber of Horrors is for the brave. For those who don't enjoy the sound of clanging chains and blood curdling screams, there is also the hall of Megastars.

For a family outing or just plain adventure, the National Wax Museum is well worth a visit.

Opening hours (All year):

Daily   10am - 6pm (last admittance 5.15pm)
Sunday   12 noon - 6pm (last admittance 5.15pm)

Potential saving - £3.50.

Based on 1996 adult admission price. (Note: 1997 savings may be even greater as many 1997 prices were not available at time of printing.)

Dublin Zoo

Phoenix Park
Dublin 8

Tel: (01) 677 1425

Present this voucher and
receive one free child
admission when accompanied
by a full-paying adult.

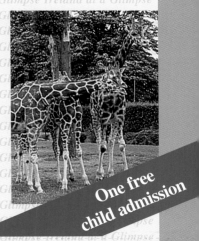

...in a changing world

Valid until 31 Dec 1997

**One free
child admission**

Phoenix Park
Visitor Centre

Phoenix Park
Dublin 8

Tel: (01) 6770095

Present this voucher and
receive one free admission
when a second of equal or
greater value is purchased.

Valid until 31 Dec 1997

**One free
admission**

Dublin Zoo

Established in 1830, Dublin Zoo is the third oldest public
Zoo in the world. The Zoo is set in 30 acres of attractive and
colourful gardens where a large collection of wild animals
and hundreds of tropical birds from around the world can be
seen. Favourite features are the new Pet Care area, "The
World of Primates" and the train ride around the Zoo.

Opening times:

Summer: March – October
Monday to Saturday	9.30 am - 6pm.
Sunday	10.30am - 6pm.

Winter: November – February
Monday to Friday	9.30am - 4pm.
Saturday	9.30am - 5pm.
Sunday and Bank Holidays	10.30 am - 5pm.

Potential saving - £3.00.

Based on 1996 admission charges for 1 child. (Note: 1997 savings may be
even greater as many 1997 prices were not available at time of printing.)

Phoenix Park Visitor Centre

Signposted from the Phoenix Monument, the tower house
which probably dates from the 17th century adjoins a visitor
centre. Here the visitor can view a historical interpretation of
the past from 3,500 B.C. to the present day. There are
exhibitions, a film show and restaurant.

Opening times:

April – May	Daily	9.30am - 5.30pm.
June – Sept	Daily	9.30am - 6.30pm.
Oct	Daily	9.30am - 5pm.

Ring **(01) 6613111** ext **2386** for winter opening hours.

Last admission 45 minutes before closing.

Opening times may change, check with site beforehand.

Potential saving - £2.00.

Based on 1996 adult admission price. (Note: 1997 savings may be even
greater as many 1997 prices were not available at time of printing.)

The Irish Whiskey Corner

Bow Street
Dublin 7

Tel: (01) 8725566

Present this voucher and receive one free admission when a second of equal or greater value is purchased.

Valid until 31 Dec 1997

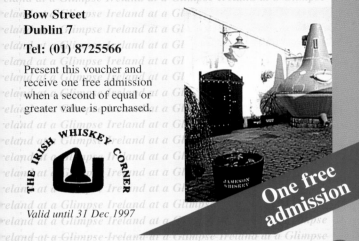

One free admission

The Dublin Experience

Trinity Conference Centre
Trinity College
Dublin 2

Tel: (01) 6081177

Present this voucher and receive one free admission when a second of equal or greater value is purchased.

The **DUBLIN** experience

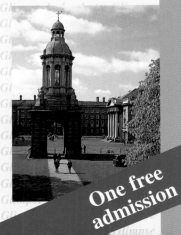

One free admission

Valid until 31 Dec 1997

The Irish Whiskey Corner

In the heart of old Dublin, just one minute's walk north of the River Liffey at Smithfield Market and nestling within an old Jameson Whiskey warehouse, is the Irish Whiskey Corner, a charming museum dedicated to the story of Irish Whiskey. Originally converted to a museum in 1984 and opened to the public the following year, the Irish Whiskey Corner has become a jewel on the Tourist Trail of Dublin.

Opening times:

May - October	Mon - Fri	Tours	11am, 2.30pm & 3.30pm.
	Sat	Tours	2.30pm & 3.30pm.
	Sun	Tours	3.30pm only.
Nov - April	Mon - Fri	Tours	3.30pm only.

Potential saving - £3.00.

Based on 1996 adult admission price. (Note: 1997 savings may be even greater as many 1997 prices were not available at time of printing.)

The Dublin Experience

This major multi-media audio-visual show, located in the Conference Centre at Trinity College, uses the most modern techniques to tell the story of Dublin. A dramatic script, stunning photography and evocative music combine to give visitors and Dubliners alike an unsurpassed introduction to the City. French, German and Italian translation are available.

Opening times:

From late May to 30 September; shows run every day, on the hour, between 10am and 5pm.

Potential saving - £3.00.

Based on 1996 adult admission price. (Note: 1997 savings may be even greater as many 1997 prices were not available at time of printing.)

Dublin Castle

Dublin

Tel: (01) 6796433

Present this voucher and receive one free admission when a second of equal or greater value is purchased.

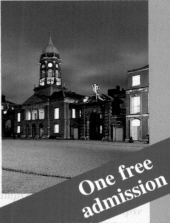

Valid until 31 Dec 1997

One free admission

Waterways Visitor Centre

Grand Canal Quay
Dublin 2
Tel: (01) 6777510

Present this voucher and receive one free admission when a second of equal or greater value is purchased.

Valid until 31 Dec 1997

One free admission

Dublin Castle

Visit Historic Dublin Castle which features:

The State Apartments - The former residential quarters of the Vice Regal Court, which are now the venue for Ireland's Presidencies of the European Union, Presidential Inaugurations and Prestigious State Functions.

The Chapel Royal - The recently restored magnificent Gothic Revival Vice Regal Church.

The Undercroft - with its unique 10th Century Viking defence encapsulated within the base of the Norman Gunpowder Tower.

(On occasions the State Apartments only may be closed for State purposes.)

Opening times:

Jan - Dec   Mon - Fri   10am - 5pm.
             Sat & Sun and Bank holidays   2pm - 5pm.
(last tour leaves 15 mins before close.)

Potential saving - £2.00.

based on 1996 Adult admission price. (Note: 1997 savings may be even greater as many 1997 prices were not available at time of printing.)

Waterways Visitor Centre

A modern building constructed in the Grand Canal Basin, beside Pearse Street Bridge and the I.D.A. Enterprise Tower. The Centre houses an exhibition designed to introduce the visitor to the story of Ireland's Inland Waterways and the range and diversity of activities and experiences they offer. Attractions include an audio-visual show and working models showing various engineering features.

Opening times:

June - September   Daily   9.30am - 6.30pm.

Potential saving - £1.50.

based on 1996 Adult admission price. (Note: 1997 savings may be even greater as many 1997 prices were not available at time of printing.)

Butterstream Gardens

Trim
Co Meath
Tel: (046) 36017

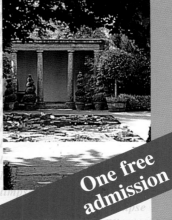

Cordially invite you to one
free admission when a second
of equal or greater value is
purchased.

Valid until 31 Dec 1997

One free admission

Athlone Castle Visitor Centre

Athlone
Co Westmeath
Tel: (0902) 72107

Cordially invite you to one
free admission when a second
of equal or greater value is
purchased.

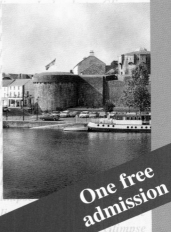

Valid until 31 Dec 1997

One free admission

Butterstream Gardens

Described by House & Garden (N.Y. July 1990) as the most imaginative garden in Ireland. Butterstream comprises a series of carefully integrated compartments which temper drama with understatement. Hedges of beech, thorn and yew frame different areas, focused on an architectural feature, an urn or a seat, where skilfully orchestrated plant themes of colour schemes enable a theatrical buildup with cool refreshing respites and unexpected surprises.

Opening times:

1 April – 30 September   Daily   11am - 6pm.

Potential saving - £3.00.

Based on 1996 adult admission price. (Note: 1997 savings may be even greater as many 1997 prices were not available at time of printing.)

Athlone Castle Visitor Centre

This 13th Century Norman Castle dominates the Town Centre and features exhibitions and audio-visual presentations on the following themes:

- Siege of Athlone.
- John Count McCormack – renowned tenor.
- River Shannon – flora and fauna.
- Folk and military museums.
- Tea rooms and art exhibitions.
- Tourist office.

This Centre is an important, unique, educational and cultural facility. Athlone – well worth a visit.

Opening times:

April – September: 10am - 6pm,
                                    and by arrangement all year

Potential saving - £2.50.

Based on 1996 adult admission price. (Note: 1997 savings may be even greater as many 1997 prices were not available at time of printing.)

Locke's Distillery Museum

Kilbeggan
Co Westmeath

Tel: (0506) 32134

Present this voucher and receive one free admission when a second of equal or greater value is purchased.

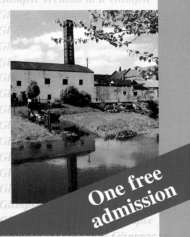

One free admission

Valid until 31 Dec 1997

Carrigglas Manor

Longford
Co Longford
Tel: (043) 45165

Cordially invite you to one free admission when a second of equal or greater value is purchased.

Carrigglas Manor

One free admission

Valid until 31 Dec 1997

Locke's Distillery Museum

Locke's Distillery was licensed in 1757 and produced whiskey for over 200 years, closing in 1953.

In 1982, the local community began restoration of the buildings to present a museum of industrial archaelology, showing the ancient process of whiskey making. Over 85% of the original machinery remains intact and restoration work is ongoing. The water wheel, powered by the Brusna river is turning once more and the whole process can be followed step by step inside the buildings.

It is the only small pot still whiskey distillery remaining in Ireland, the only example of what used to be a widespread Irish industry. The tour is complemented by the tales and stories gathered from the workers from the distillery.

Opening times:

November to March	10am - 4pm
April to October	9am - 6pm

Potential saving - £2.00.

Based on 1996 adult admission price. (Note: 1997 savings may be even greater as many 1997 prices were not available at time of printing.)

Carrigglas Manor

A fine Gothic Revival Manor House still in original private ownership and set in extensive parkland. Enjoy a personal guided tour through the romantic interiors of the house. Magnificent Georgian double courtyard by James Gandon, being restored at present. Charming tiered woodland garden, costume museum, tea room and Victorian gift shop. Self-catering and private accommodation also available, May – October inclusive.

Opening times:

1 June - 1 Sept   1.30pm - 5.30pm (Aug 6pm) except Tues and Wed.

Open Sundays 2pm to 6pm.

Potential saving - £4.00.

Based on 1996 adult admission price to the House, Museum and Gardens. (Note: 1997 savings may be even greater as many 1997 prices were not available at time of printing.)

Corlea Trackway Visitor Centre

Kenagh
Co Longford

Tel: (043) 22386

Present this voucher and receive one free admission when a second of equal or greater value is purchased.

One free admission

Valid until 31 Dec 1997

Killykeen Forest Park

Killykeen
Co Cavan

Tel: (049) 32541

Present this voucher and receive one free admission when a second of equal or greater value is purchased. This offer does not extend to the residential accommodation.

One free admission

coillte

Valid until 31 Dec 1997

Corlea Trackway Visitor Centre

The centre interprets the timber trackway which dates from 147 B.C. and was found underneath the bog during turf cutting operations.

Opening times:

June - September   Daily   9.30 am - 6.30 pm.

Ring **(01) 6613111** ext **2386** for off season opening hours. Opening times may change, check with site beforehand.

Last admission 45 minutes before closing.

Potential saving - £2.50.

Based on 1996 adult admission price. (Note: 1997 savings may be even greater as many 1997 prices were not available at time of printing.)

Killykeen Forest Park

Killykeen comprises some 250 hectares of mixed woodland on the Erne river system. The park formed part of the former Farnham Estate, and the main features of interest include Killykeen Cottage, Clough Oughter Castle and a variety of archaeological remains. A unique self-catering complex, constructed entirely of Irish-grown timber, has been developed within the park. It includes chalets and log cabins, equestrian centre, conference centre and a range of activities. For day visitors, there is excellent coarse fishing, pony trekking, forest walks and nature trails. The range of habitat types encourages a rich diversity of wildlife.

Opening times:

Open all day every day throughout the year.

Potential saving - £1.00.

Based on 1996 adult admission price. (Note: 1997 savings may be even greater as many 1997 prices were not available at time of printing.)

Carraig Craft Visitors' Centre

Mountnugent
Co Cavan

Tel: (049) 40179

Cordially invites you and your
guest to enjoy one
complimentary admission
when a second
of equal or
greater value
is purchased.

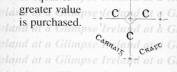

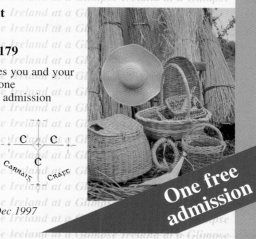

Valid until 31 Dec 1997

One free admission

St Kilian's Heritage Centre

Mullagh
Co Cavan

Tel: (046) 42433

Present this voucher and
receive one free admission
when a second of equal or
greater value is purchased.

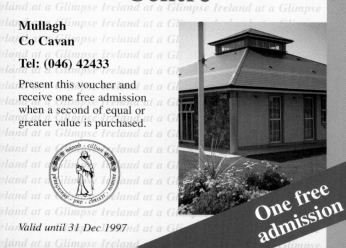

Valid until 31 Dec 1997

One free admission

Carraig Craft Visitors' Centre

The Visitor Centre lies one mile outside the pretty village of Mountnugent, surrounded on all sides by countryside steeped in history and folklore. The centre includes:

Rod and Rush Basketry.
Corn Dollies.
Craft Workshops.
Lectures and Demonstrations.
Basketry Museum with Audio Visual Presentation.

Facilities available include a coffee shop, tourist information and a local tour guide service.

Opening times:

All Year: Monday to Saturday   10am - 6pm.

              Sunday   2 pm - 6pm.

Potential saving - £2.00.

Based on 1996 adult admission price. (Note: 1997 savings may be even greater as many 1997 prices were not available at time of printing.)

St Kilian's Heritage Centre

St Kilian born Mullagh c.640, set sail from Kenmare Harbour, Kerry c.680. Leaving behind his homeland he followed the Rhine and Maine to Wurzburg city c.685. The ruler of the locality Duke Gosbert was converted to Christianity, but married his brother's wife, Geilana, contrary to Church Law and Kilian ordered them to separate. In revenge Geilana had Kilian and two of his companions beheaded and their bodies secretly buried. Years later their bodies were discovered and in c.752 were later enshrined in Wurzburg Cathedral. From this time on the Kilian cult grew. Today devotion to St Kilian is as strong as ever in Wurzburg and Ireland.

Opening times:

Easter - October (Inclusive):
              Monday - Saturday   10am - 6pm.
              Sunday   12.30 pm - 6pm.

Potential saving - £2.00.

Based on 1996 adult admission price. (Note: 1997 savings may be even greater as many 1997 prices were not available at time of printing.)

Lough Rynn Estate

Mohill
Co Leitrim

Tel: (078) 31427

Present this voucher and receive one free admission when a second of equal or greater value is purchased.

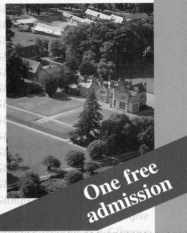

Valid until 31 Dec 1997

One free admission

Patrick Kavanagh rural & literary resource centre

Inniskeen
Co Monaghan

Tel: (042) 78560

Present this voucher and receive one free admission when a second of equal or greater value is purchased. (Note - offer also applies to the Kavanagh Country Tour for which advance booking is essential.)

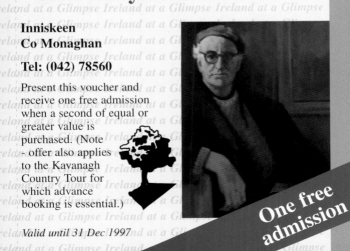

Valid until 31 Dec 1997

One free admission

Lough Rynn Estate

Lough Rynn Estate has, for two centuries, been the seat of the Clements family, Earls of Leitrim. The third Earl, William Sydney Clements, is regarded as the principal architect of the Demesne and the legacy of his stewardship of 40 years may be witnessed today in the buildings and gardens. It was his assassination in 1878 which effectively heralded the demise of landlordism in the latter part of the last century. The estate comprises 100 acres of woodland, ornamental gardens an open pasture and 600 acres of lake.

Other facilities available include restaurant/craft shop, picnic site and playground

Opening times:

May - End of August   10am - 7pm

Potential saving - £1.25.

Based on 1996 adult admission price. (Note: 1997 savings may be even greater as many 1997 prices were not available at time of printing.)

Patrick Kavanagh rural & literary resource centre

Housed in the Parish Church immortalised by Kavanagh's classic novel 'Tarry Flynn' the Centre blends the rich heritage of South Ulster with life in turn-of-the-Century rural Ireland, as seen through the eyes and words of Ireland's foremost 20th Century literary figure and character about Dublin, Patrick Kavanagh. Kavanagh's rolling hills and intimate fields provide an evocative backdrop for the unique Kavanagh Country Tour, as a local actor takes visitors around the sites made famous in verse, adding anecdotes, excerpts from Tarry Flynn and The Green Fool, a hint of 'insider' information, the obligatory wild rumours and even the odd poem!

Opening times:

1 June - 30 Sept	Weekdays	11am - 5pm.
	Weekends & Holidays	2pm - 6pm.
1 Oct - 31 May	Weekdays	11am - 5pm.
Sundays & Holidays	**Except** 1 Dec - 16 Mar	2 pm - 6pm.
(Closed Saturdays.)		

Potential saving - £3.00.

Based on 1996 adult admission price for the tour. (Note: 1997 savings may be even greater as many 1997 prices were not available at time of printing.)

Ulster Canal Stores

Clones
Co Monaghan
Tel: (047) 52125/51718

Present this voucher and
receive one free admission
when a second of equal or
greater value is purchased.

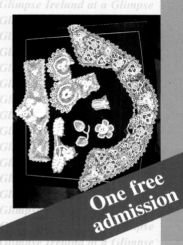

Valid until 31 Dec 1997

One free admission

Galway Irish Crystal Heritage Centre

Merlin Park
Galway
Tel: (091) 757311

Present this voucher and
receive one free admission
when a second of equal or
greater value is purchased.

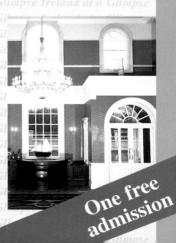

Galway
IRISH CRYSTAL

Valid until 31 Dec 1997

One free admission

Ulster Canal Stores

This restored 18th century stone canal warehouse contains a uniquely mounted history of a hand-craft established during the Great Famine as a 'relief scheme' and revived now by a local co-op. It is exported world-wide and is represented in the White House and Buckingham Palace. Lace and other crafts are on sale. This is also a tourist information point and the starting place for walking, cycling and town trails in a verdant countryside rich in history and heritage. Famous sons include Sir Thomas Lipton, Boxer Barry McGuigan and playwrights Eugene and Pat McCabe whose recent novels include Death and Nightingales and Butcher Boy (a Warner Brothers film). Cycle hire available.

Opening times:

June - September	Mon - Sat	10am - 6pm.
	Sun	2pm - 6pm.

Potential saving - £1.50.

based on 1996 Adult admission price (Note: 1997 savings may be even greater as many 1997 prices were not available at time of printing.)

Galway Irish Crystal Heritage Centre

A visit to the impressive Galway Irish Crystal Heritage Centre provides visitors with an excellent introduction to the rich history and culture of the West of Ireland. Learn about the craft process at Galway Irish Crystal and see how the heritage of Galway has inspired crafts-people for decades.

Facilities at the Heritage Centre are excellent and include the Great Hall with its sweeping double staircase and magnificent chandelier, a spacious balcony overlooking Galway Bay, a relaxing restaurant and extensive showroom. Guided tours of the centre run every 30 minutes.

Opening times:

May - September	Mon - Fri	8am - 8pm.
	Sat	9am - 6pm.
	Sun	10am - 6pm.
October - April	Mon - Fri	9am - 6pm.
	Sat & Sun	10am - 6pm.

Potential saving - £1.50.

based on 1996 Adult admission price. (Note: 1997 savings may be even greater as many 1997 prices were not available at time of printing.)

Kylemore Abbey

Connemara
Co Galway
Tel: (095) 41146

Cordially invite you to one
free admission when a second
of equal or greater value is
purchased.

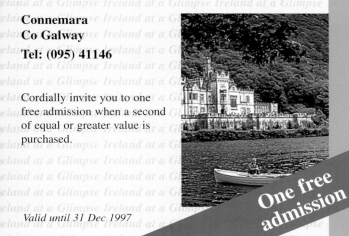

Valid until 31 Dec 1997

One free
admission

Leenane Cultural Centre

Leenane
Co Galway
Tel: (095) 42323/42231

Present this voucher and we
will allow you one free
admission when a second of
equal or greater value is
purchased.

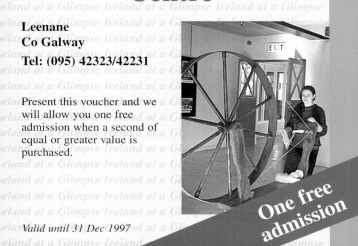

Valid until 31 Dec 1997

One free
admission

Kylemore Abbey

Kylemore Abbey, home of the Irish Benedictine nuns, is situated at the foot of the twelve Ben mountains overlooking Pollnacappul Lake. It was built as a private residence in 1868, by Michael Henry, as a gift for his wife. The architecture is Neo-Gothic and the house displays all of the decorative features of the period. The newly-restored Gothic church is the jewel in the crown of Kylemore, and it is well worth a visit. Relax in the restaurant and visit the craft shop run and managed by the nuns. Discover the past and present life of the Abbey/Castle in our visitor centre.

Opening times:

17 March – October   Open daily: 09.30am - 5.45pm.

Potential saving - £1.50.

Based on 1996 adult admission price. (Note: 1997 savings may be even greater as many 1997 prices were not available at time of printing.)

Leenane Cultural Centre

This beautifully-situated centre interprets the local sheep and wool industry, and overlooks Killary's lovely natural harbour. Wool handcrafts, including carding, spinning, weaving and the use of natural dyes are all demonstrated. Over 20 different breeds of sheep graze on the lands around the house. Local history and places of interest are featured on a continuous audio-visual display.

Opening times:

April 1 – End of October. Open 10am - 6pm every day.

Potential saving - £2.00.

Based on 1996 adult admission price. (Note: 1997 savings may be even greater as many 1997 prices were not available at time of printing.)

Coole

Gort
Co Galway
Tel: (091) 631804

Present this voucher and
receive one free admission
when a second of equal or
greater value is purchased.

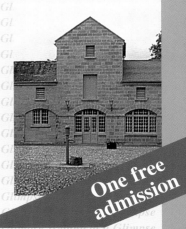

One free admission

Valid until 31 Dec 1997

Foxford Woollen Mills Visitor Centre

Foxford
Co Mayo
Tel: (094) 56756

Cordially invites you and your
guest to enjoy one
complimentary admission
when a second of equal or
greater value is purchased.

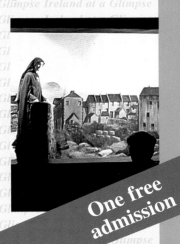

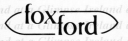

One free admission

Valid until 31 Dec 1997

Coole

Coole Park was the home of Lady Augusta Gregory, dramatist and co-founder with Edward Martyn and WB Yeats of the Abbey Theatre. Attractions include an audio-visual show, exhibitions, nature trails, walks, the famous 'autograph tree', a lake, turlough and tearooms.

Opening times:

Mid April – mid June	Tues – Sun	10am - 5pm.
	Closed Mon.	
Mid June – end August	Daily	9.30am - 6.30pm.
September	Daily	10am - 5pm.

Last admission 45 minutes before closing.

Opening times may change, check with site beforehand.

Potential saving - £2.00.

Based on 1996 adult admission price. (Note: 1997 savings may be even greater as many 1997 prices were not available at time of printing.)

Foxford Woollen Mills Visitor Centre

The Visitor Centre traces the success story of this remarkable mill from its humble beginnings by a nun to the thriving craft industry it is today. The story is told through a multi-lingual historical presentation, followed by a tour of the working mills where skilled crafts people still produce the famous Foxford blankets, rugs and tweeds. Shop and restaurant also open.

Opening times:

May – October	Mon – Sat:	10am - 6pm.
	Sunday:	12 noon - 6pm.
November – April	Mon – Sat:	10am - 6pm.
	Sunday:	2pm - 6pm.

Average length of visit: one-hour tours every 20 minutes.

Potential saving - £3.00.

Based on 1996 adult admission price. (Note: 1997 savings may be even greater as many 1997 prices were not available at time of printing.)

Westport House

**Westport
Co Mayo**

Tel: (098) 25430

Present this voucher and receive one free admission when a second of equal or greater value is purchased.

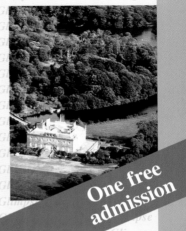

One free admission

Valid until 31 Dec 1997

Strokestown Park House, Museum and Gardens

**Strokestown
Co Roscommon**

Tel: (078) 33013

Cordially invite you and your guest to enjoy one complimentary admission when a second of equal or greater value is purchased.

One free admission

Valid until 31 Dec 1997

Westport House

An inclusive ticket can be bought to give access to the Aladdin's Cave of wonderful attractions which lie within the Westport House Country Estate. This is a destination for all the family. Those interested in history can enjoy the graceful lines and period furnishings of 17th century Westport House, designed by Richard Castle. The estate, developed over 30 years, now carries a cornucopia of pleasurable activities. These include children's zoo, ball pond, pitch & putt, playground, boating, antique shop, art centre, miniature railway, hill slide, slippery dip, model railway, dungeons, supabounce, pinkie rabbit and old kitchen tea room.

Opening times:

May - mid September   Daily.

Telephone **(098) 25430/27766** for details.

Potential saving - £6.50.

Based on 1996 Adult admission price to Westport House and Children's Zoo. (Note: 1997 savings may be even greater as many 1997 prices were not available at time of printing.)

Strokestown Park House, Museum and Gardens

Strokestown Park House was constructed for Thomas Mahon MP in the 1740s. Built in the Palladian style, the house is complete with its original contents and has good examples of 18th and 19th Century interiors. The stable yards of the house have been converted into Ireland's first museum commemorating the Great Irish Famine of the 1840's and the newly restored gardens are now open to the public.
Restaurant facilities also available.

Opening times:

Easter - 31 October

Tuesday - Sunday   11am - 5.30pm.

CLOSED MONDAY.

Potential saving - £6.95.

Based on 1996 adult admission price to the House, Museum and Gardens. (Note: 1997 savings may be even greater as many 1997 prices were not available at time of printing.)

King House

Boyle
Co Roscommon

Tel: (79) 63243

Present this voucher and
receive one free admission
when a second of equal or
greater value is purchased..

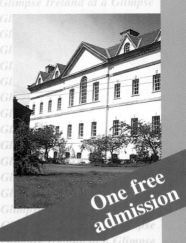

Valid until 31 Dec 1997

One free admission

Tullyboy Animal Farm

Tullyboy
Boyle
Co Roscommon

Tel: (079) 68031

Cordially invite you to one
free admission when a second
of equal or greater value is
purchased.

Valid until 31 Dec 1997

One free admission

King House

King House, built by Sir Henry King around 1730, is a house of unique architectural and historic importance. It was home to the King family until 1788 when it became a military barracks and was the home of the famous Connaught Rangers regiment and latterly the National Army.

Now magnificently restored King House contains several entertaining and informative exhibitions. The story of the ancient Kingdom of Connacht and the King family history are explored. Further areas focus on the many battles and triumphs of the Connaught Rangers Regiment and the achievements of the lengthy restoration programme.

Opening times:

April	Sat & Sun	10am - 6pm.
May - September	Daily	10am - 6pm.
October	Sat & Sun	10am - 6pm.

Last admission 5pm.

Potential saving - £3.00.

Based on 1996 adult admission price. (Note: 1997 savings may be even greater as many 1997 prices were not available at time of printing.)

Tullyboy Animal Farm

Set in a beautiful location with views of the Curlew and Arigna Mountains, Tullyboy Animal Farm is centred around an 18th Century farmhouse. The open farm introduces the family to caring country life. With 8,500 sq ft under cover you can enjoy the farm in any weather. Pony rides, Ostriches, Llamas, Pets Corner, duck pond, playground and picnic area are other attractions. A gift shop offers a variety of quality crafts and the old world tearooms are an ideal place to catch your breath. R.D.S/Bord Failte approved.

Opening times:

May – September	Mon - Sat	10.30am - 6pm.
	Sun	12 noon - 6pm.

Potential saving - £2.00.

Based on 1996 adult admission price. (Note: 1997 savings may be even greater as many 1997 prices were not available at time of printing.)

Lissadell House

Drumcliffe
Co Sligo

Tel: (071) 63150

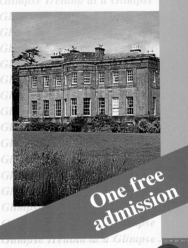

Present this voucher and we
will give you one free
admission when a second of
equal or greater value is
purchased.

**One free
admission**

Valid until 31 Dec 1997

Ionad Cois Locha

Dunlewey
Letterkenny
Co Donegal

Tel: (075) 31699

Cordially invite you to one
free admission when a second
of equal or greater value is
purchased.

**One free
admission**

Valid until 31 Dec 1997

Lissadell House

Lissadell - "That Old Georgian Mansion" in the words of W. B. Yeats - is still owned and lived in by the Gore-Booth family. Childhood home of the Countess Markievich, it is full of furniture, pictures and artefacts associated with succeeding generations of the family. Visitors will experience the genuine atmosphere of the faded grandeur of times gone by.

Opening times:

1 June – mid September.

Monday – Saturday   10.30am - 12.15pm.

2pm - 4.15pm.

CLOSED ON SUNDAY.

Potential saving - £2.50.

Based on 1996 adult admission price. (Note: 1997 savings may be even greater as many 1997 prices were not available at time of printing.)

Ionad Cois Locha

Award-winning centre at the foot of Mount Errigal. Home of the famous weaver 'Manus Ferry'. Demonstrations in carding, spinning and weaving of wool. Guided tours of the restored house and farm, storytelling boat trips on Dunlewey Lake. Adventure play area, pet animals. Restaurant, tea room and craft shop. Eist le Gaeilge agus labhair i.

Opening times:

16 March – 30 March:	Sat:	10.30am - 6pm.
	Sunday:	11am - 7pm.
31 March – 4 November:	Mon – Sat:	10.30am - 6pm.
	Sunday:	11am - 7pm.

Potential saving - £4.00.

Based on 1996 adult admission price, including Tour of the Weaver's Cottage, Cruise on the lake and admission to the farm. (Note: 1997 savings may be even greater as many 1997 prices were not available at time of printing.)

Cavanacor Historic House and Craft Centre

Ballindrait
Lifford
Co Donegal

Tel: (074) 41143

Cordially invite you to one
free admission when a second
of equal or greater value is
purchased.

Valid until 31 Dec 1997

One free admission

Lifford Old Courthouse Visitors Centre

Foyle View
Lifford
Co Donegal

Tel: (074) 41228/41733

Present this voucher and
receive one free admission
when a second of equal
or greater value
is purchased.

The Old Courthouse

Valid until 31 Dec 1997

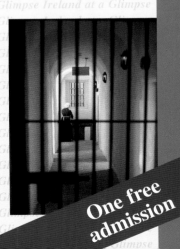

One free admission

Cavanacor Historic House and Craft Centre

Set in 10 acres of landscaped grounds, Cavanacor House was built in the early 1600's and is the ancestral home of James Knox Polk, 11th president of the USA. King James II dined here on 20 April 1689. The house is furnished in Jacobean and Georgian style. Museum, art gallery, craft shop, tearoom, walled garden and working pottery in fortified yard.

Opening times:

Easter, June, July, August: Tues – Sat: 12 noon - 6pm.
                             Sun: 2pm - 6pm.

Closed Mondays, except Bank Holidays.

Potential saving - £2.50.

Based on 1996 adult admission price. (Note: 1997 savings may be even greater as many 1997 prices were not available at time of printing.)

Lifford Old Courthouse Visitors Centre

Reach into the Past & Relive the harrowing experiences of prisoners awaiting trial in the superbly restored 18th Century Courthouse.

- Manus O'Donnell Audio Visual of the Chieftains of Ireland.
- Re-enacted famous Trials in the Courtroom Scene eg Napper Tandy.
- Storyboard Area with Visuals and Artefacts.
- Down below - damp, dark dungeons.
- Clans Room with famous Donegal Names.
- Relax and enjoy our Coffee Dock and Gift Shop.

Opening times:

March 17th - Easter	Saturday	10am - 6 pm.
	Sunday	2pm - 6pm.
Easter - October 31st	Monday - Saturday	10am - 6pm.
	Sunday	2pm - 6pm.

Potential saving - £2.50.

Based on 1996 adult admission price. (Note: 1997 savings may be even greater as many 1997 prices were not available at time of printing.)

Marble Arch Caves

Marlbank Scenic Loop
Florencecourt
Co Fermanagh

Tel: (01365) 348855

Present this voucher and
receive one free admission
when a second of equal or
greater value is purchased.

...A District Council Service

Valid until 31 Dec 1997

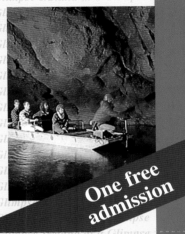

One free admission

Belleek Pottery & Visitors Centre

Belleek
Co Fermanagh

Tel: (013656) 58501

Cordially invite you to one
free admission when a second
of equal or greater value is
purchased.

Valid until 31 Dec 1997

One free admission

Marble Arch Caves

Deep under Cuilcagh Mountain in south west Fermanagh, 3 small underground rivers have carved out a spectacular world of caves during the past 300 million years. Explore this magical underground on boat and foot following the route of the early cavers.

Opening times:

The caves are open 7 days a week,
31 March – 30 September;

10.30am to 4.30pm (5pm in July and August). The caves can be affected by heavy rain; please phone to ensure availability of tour.

Potential saving - £5.00.

Based on 1996 adult admission price. (Note: 1997 savings may be even greater as many 1997 prices were not available at time of printing.)

Belleek Pottery & Visitors Centre

On the banks of the River Erne, set right in the heart of the Fermanagh Lake Lands lies Belleek, home of Ireland's oldest pottery. For more than 137 years, this little village has been famous for its distinctive parian china. Today, the magnificent pottery building is also home to the Belleek Visitors Centre and each year thousands of people leave the hustle of modern life behind to immerse themselves in the Belleek experience. Guided Pottery Tours, Museum, Audio-visual Theatre, Restaurant and Shop.

Opening times: (Note – tours only operate Mon-Fri.)

	Mon–Fri.	Saturday.	Sunday.
March–June	9am - 6pm.	10am - 6pm.	2pm - 6pm.
July & August	9am - 8pm.	10am - 6pm.	11am - 8pm.
September	9am - 6pm.	10am - 6pm.	2pm - 6pm.
October	9am - 5pm.	10am - 5.30pm.	2pm - 6pm.
November	9am - 5.30pm.	CLOSED.	CLOSED.

Potential saving - £1.00.

Based on 1996 adult admission price. (Note: 1997 savings may be even greater as many 1997 prices were not available at time of printing.)

Florence Court

Florence Court
Co Fermanagh
Tel: (01365) 348249

Cordially invites you and your
guest to enjoy one complimentary
ADMISSION when a second
ADMISSION of equal or greater
value is purchased.

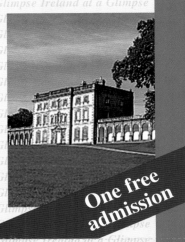

🌺 The National Trust

Valid until 31 Dec 1997,
during published opening times.
Not valid for special events.

One free admission

Castle Coole

Enniskillen
Co Fermanagh
Tel: (01365) 322690

Cordially invites you and your
guest to enjoy one complimentary
ADMISSION when a second
ADMISSION of equal or greater
value is purchased.

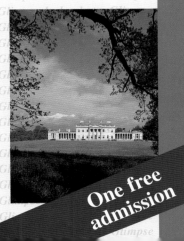

🌺 The National Trust

Valid until 31 Dec 1997,
during published opening times.
Not valid for special events.

One free admission

Florence Court

One of the most important houses in Ulster, built in the middle of the Eighteenth Century by John Cole, father of 1st Earl of Enniskillen; fine Rococo plasterwork; pleasure grounds with ice house and water-powered sawmill. Fine views over surrounding mountains. Walled garden. Collection of Irish furniture. Rebuilt Summer House in the Pleasure Grounds.

Opening times:

April and Sept – Sat, Sun and Bank Holidays:
1pm - 6pm.

Easter (March 28th - April 1st)

Daily 1pm - 6pm.

May – August Daily (except Tues) 1pm - 6pm.

Potential saving - £2.60.

Based on 1996 adult admission price. (Note: 1997 savings may be even greater as many 1997 prices were not available at time of printing.)

Castle Coole

Superb late Eighteenth Century neo-Classical house designed by James Wyatt, family home of the Earls of Belmore. A visit can now include the ornate State Bedroom, the Servants' Tunnel, five of the original stables in the Grand Yard and the Belmore Private Coach, in its original coach house.

Opening times:

April and Sept; Sat, Sun and Bank Holidays:
1pm - 6pm.

Easter (March 28th - April 1st)

Daily 1pm - 6pm.

May – August Daily (except Thurs) 1pm - 6pm.

Potential saving - £2.60.

Based on 1996 adult admission price. (Note: 1997 savings may be even greater as many 1997 prices were not available at time of printing.)

Enniskillen Castle

Castle Barracks
Enniskillen
Co Fermanagh

Tel: (01365) 325000

Present this voucher and
receive one free admission
when a second of equal
or greater value
is purchased.

Valid until 31 Dec 1997

One free admission

Ulster American Folk Park

Mellon Road
Omagh
Co Tyrone
Tel: (01662) 243292

Cordially invite you to a free
admission when a second of
equal or greater value is
purchased.

*Not applicable
to Educational
Visits (Schools)
or Special Events*

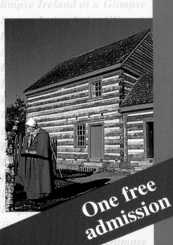

Valid until 31 Dec 1997

One free admission

Enniskillen Castle

A family attraction on the banks of the River Erne, your visit to Enniskillen Castle includes the Heritage Centre, Museum of the Royal Inniskiling fusiliers and displays around the castle yard. Award-winning displays guide you through the wetlands of Fermanagh following the progression from early farming techniques to the establishment of industries such as Belleek Pottery. New displays can be explored in the yard, with models of life in the 15th and 17th centuries in the vaults of the old Castle Keep. Facilities include: gift and bookshop, children's activity corners, exhibition programme, audio-visual theatre, refreshments.

Opening times:

May, June, September:	Monday & Saturday	2pm - 5pm.
	Tuesday - Friday	10am - 5pm.
July & August as above plus Sunday		2pm - 5pm.
1 October - 30 April:	Monday	2pm - 5pm.
	Tuesday - Friday	10am - 5pm.

Potential saving - £2.00.

Based on 1996 adult admission price. (Note: 1997 savings may be even greater as many 1997 prices were not available at time of printing.)

Ulster American Folk Park

This is an outdoor museum designed to tell the story of the great waves of emigrants who left Ulster for the New World in the 18th and 19th Centuries, and of the contribution they made to the USA throughout the whole period of its birth and development. Through its unique display of outdoor exhibits, featuring many original buildings such as the ancestral homes of Thomas Mellon, John Joseph Hughes and Hugh & Robert Campbell, the Ulster American Folk Park depicts the varied aspects of emigrants' life and experience on both sides of the Atlantic during the 18th and 19th Centuries.

Opening times:

Easter – September:	
Monday – Saturday	11am - 6.30pm.
Sundays/Public Holidays	11.30am - 7pm.
October – Easter:	
Monday – Friday	10.30am - 5pm.

Closed Saturdays, Sundays and Public Holidays.

Potential saving - £3.50.

Based on 1996 adult admission price. (Note: 1997 savings may be even greater as many 1997 prices were not available at time of printing.)

The Ulster History Park

Cullion
Omagh
Co Tyrone

Tel: (016626) 48188

Cordially invite you to a free
admission when a second of
equal or greater value is
purchased. Special events
excluded.

THE
ULSTER
HISTORY
PARK

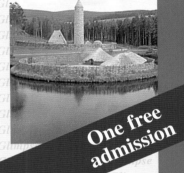

One free admission

Valid until 31 Dec 1997

Tyrone Crystal

Killybrackey
Dungannon
Co Tyrone

Tel: (01868) 725335

Present this voucher and
receive one free admission
when a second of equal or
greater value is purchased.

Tyrone Crystal

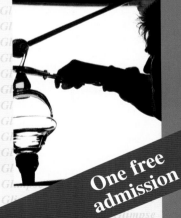

One free admission

Valid until 31 Dec 1997

The Ulster History Park

Take a trail through time from the Stone Age to the Plantations. Explore full-scale models of homes and monuments which illustrate the history of settlement in Ireland through 10,000 years. A multi-media audio-visual programme and exhibition of artefacts, models and illustrations expand the theme.

Opening times:

April – September	Mon – Sat:	10.30am - 6.30pm.
	Sunday	11.30am - 7pm.
	Public holidays	10.30am - 7pm.
October – March	Mon – Fri	10.30am - 5pm.

Last admission $1^1/_2$ hours before closing.

Potential saving - £3.00.

Based on 1996 adult admission price. (Note: 1997 savings may be even greater as many 1997 prices were not available at time of printing.)

Tyrone Crystal

Each piece of Tyrone Crystal is individually mouth blown and hand-cut. The production process is fascinating and one which attracts visitors from all over the world. Specially trained tour guides allow visitors to inspect the cutting and blowing craftsmen at close quarters. Following a factory tour, visitors are invited to browse round the Craft Centre or enjoy a snack in the Coffee Shop. Tours do not need to be pre-booked but a quick phone call will ensure that your tour will be given priority.

Opening times:

All Year Monday - Saturday 9am - 5pm.

Tours are available: (Scheduled every 30 minutes.)
Monday - Thursday & Saturday 9.30 am - 3.30 pm.
Friday 9.30 am - 12.00 noon.

Potential saving - £2.00.

Based on 1996 adult admission price. (Note: 1997 savings may be even greater as many 1997 prices were not available at time of printing.)

Wellbrook Beetling Mill

Corkhill, Cookstown
Co Tyrone

Tel: (016487) 51735

Cordially invites you and your
guest to enjoy one complimentary
ADMISSION when a second
ADMISSION of equal or greater
value is purchased.

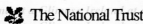 The National Trust

Valid until 31 Dec 1997,
during published opening times.
Not valid for special events.

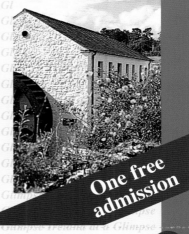

One free admission

The Argory

Derrycaw Road
Moy, Dungannon
Co Tyrone

Tel: (018687) 84753

Cordially invites you and your
guest to enjoy one complimentary
ADMISSION when a second
ADMISSION of equal or greater
value is purchased.

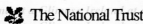 The National Trust

Valid until 31 Dec 1997,
during published opening times.
Not valid for special events.

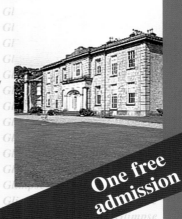

One free admission

Wellbrook Beetling Mill

A hammer mill powered by water for beetling – the final process in linen manufacturing; original machinery in working order; situated in attractive glen; wooded walks along the Ballinderry River and by the mill race (always open).

Opening times:

April, May, June and Sept; Sat, Sun and Bank Holidays:
2pm - 6pm.

Easter (March 28th - April 1st)
Daily   2pm - 6pm.

July and August   Daily (except Tues)   2pm - 6pm.

Potential saving - £1.50.

Based on 1996 adult admission price. (Note: 1997 savings may be even greater as many 1997 prices were not available at time of printing.)

The Argory

Set in 315 acres of wooded countryside, overlooking the River Blackwater, the house dates from 1824 but is substantially unchanged since the turn of the century; fascinating furniture and interesting contents which include an 1824 organ; the imposing stable yard includes a coach house, harness room, laundry and acetylene gas plant. Charming sundial garden; extensive walks; playground.

Opening times:

April, May and Sept; Sat, Sun and Bank Holidays:
2pm - 6pm.

Easter (March 28th - April 1st)
Daily   2pm - 6pm.

June – August   Daily (except Tuesday)   2pm - 6pm.

(Open from 1pm on Bank Holidays.)

Potential saving - £2.30.

Based on 1996 adult admission price. (Note: 1997 savings may be even greater as many 1997 prices were not available at time of printing.)

Gray's Printing Press

49 Main Street
Strabane
Co Tyrone

Tel: (01504) 884094

Cordially invite you and your
guest to enjoy one complimentary
ADMISSION when a second
ADMISSION of equal or greater
value is purchased.

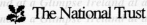 The National Trust

Valid until 31 Dec 1997,
during published opening times.
Not valid for special events.

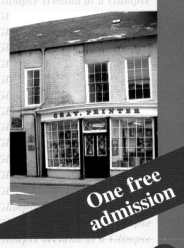

One free
admission

An Creagán
Visitor Centre

Creggan
Omagh
Co Tyrone

Tel: (016627) 61112

Present this voucher and
receive one free admission
when a second of equal or
greater value is purchased.

MID ULSTER ENTERPRISES
— CREGGAN LIMITED —

Valid until 31 Dec 1997

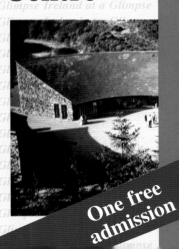

One free
admission

Gray's Printing Press

Eighteenth Century printing press, shop and stationers; collection of Nineteenth Century hand printing machines; "The Power of Print" audio visual display brings the story of printing to life.

Opening times:

April – Sept; daily except Thurs, Sun and Bank Holidays: 2pm - 5.30pm.

At other times by prior arrangement.

Shop – Open all year; daily except Thurs, Sun and Bank Holidays: 9am - 1pm and 2pm - 5.30pm.

Potential saving - £1.50.

Based on 1996 adult admission price. (Note: 1997 savings may be even greater as many 1997 prices were not available at time of printing.)

An Creagán Visitor Centre

Experience the educational and entertaining interpretative exhibition featuring the area's rich geographical and archaeological remains. With forty four archaelogical sites within a five mile radius, including wedge tombs, portal tombs, court tombs, stone circles and standing stones, virtually every type of ancient monument is represented. The Black Bog, an Area of Special Scientific Interest, and one of the largest raised bogs in Ireland is just a mile away, so there is plenty to see. The many structured walks and cycle routes are designed to incorporate the bog trails, archaeological sites, a 40's and 50's restored traditional farm and the spectacular landscapes.

Opening times:

1 April - 30 September   Every Day   11am - 6.30 pm.

1 October - 31 March   Monday - Friday   11am - 4.30 pm.

Potential saving - £2.00.

Based on 1996 adult admission price. (Note: 1997 savings may be even greater as many 1997 prices were not available at time of printing.)

Tower Museum

Union Hall Place
Derry
Co Derry

Tel: (01504) 372411

Present this voucher and we will
allow you one free admission
when a second of equal or greater
value is purchased.

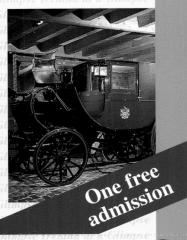

TOWER
MUSEUM

Valid until 31 Dec 1997

One free admission

Springhill

Moneymore
Magherafelt
Co Londonderry

Tel: (016487) 48210

Cordially invites you and your
guest to enjoy one complimentary
ADMISSION when a second
ADMISSION of equal or greater
value is purchased.

 The National Trust

Valid until 31 Dec 1997,
during published opening times.
Not valid for special events.

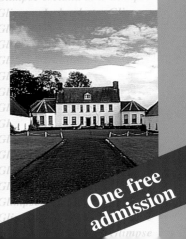

One free admission

Tower Museum

The Tower Museum is a comprehensive, award-winning display outlining the dramatic and turbulent history of the City of Derry from prehistoric times to the present day. It utilises the most modern presentation techniques, including a wide range of audio-visual programmes, theatrical devices and original historical and archaeological artefacts from all periods of the city's history.

Opening times:

Jan to June, Sept to Dec   10am - 5pm Tues - Sat.
July and August   10am - 5pm Mon - Sat
                   2pm - 5pm Sun.

All Bank Holiday.
Mondays   10am - 5pm.

Potential saving - £2.75.

Based on 1996 adult admission price. (Note: 1997 savings may be even greater as many 1997 prices were not available at time of printing.)

Springhill

Seventeenth Century whitewashed house with mid-eighteenth and early nineteenth century additions; it contains family furniture, paintings, ornaments and curios. The extensive outbuildings (two in the Dutch style flanking the mansion, and a fortified barn dating from the Seventeenth Century) house an extensive costume collection; secluded walled gardens and woodland walks.

Opening times:

April, May and Sept; Sat, Sun and Bank Holidays:
                                           2pm - 6pm.

Easter (March 28th - April 1st)
            Daily   2pm - 6pm.

June – August   Daily (except Thursday)   2pm - 6pm.

Potential saving - £2.30.

Based on 1996 adult admission price. (Note: 1997 savings may be even greater as many 1997 prices were not available at time of printing.)

Hezlett House

107 Sea Road
Castlerock
Co Londonderry
Tel: (01265) 848567

Cordially invite you and your
guest to enjoy one complimentary
ADMISSION when a second
ADMISSION of equal or greater
value is purchased.

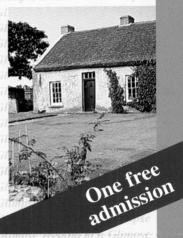

 The National Trust

Valid until 31 Dec 1997,
during published opening times.
Not valid for special events.

One free admission

Old Bushmills Distillery

Bushmills
Co Antrim
Tel: (012657) 33218

Present this voucher and we
will allow you one free
admission when a second of
equal or greater value is
purchased.

Valid until 31 Dec 1997

One free admission

Hezlett House

Seventeenth century thatched cottage, important because of the cruck truss construction of the roof. Now furnished in late Victorian style. Small museum of farm implements.

Opening times:

April, May, June and Sept; Sat, Sun and Public Holidays:
1pm - 6pm.

Easter (March 28th - April 1st)
Daily   1pm - 6pm.

July and August   Daily (except Tues)   1pm - 6pm.

Potential saving - £1.50.

Based on 1996 adult admission price. (Note: 1997 savings may be even greater as many 1997 prices were not available at time of printing.)

Old Bushmills Distillery

This is the world's oldest whiskey Distillery and has been in business since 1608. Visitors accompany their guide through the many stages in the age-old art of whiskey making and finish with a taste of the product. Other facilities include: gift, whiskey and coffee shop.

Opening times:

March - October   Daily   9.30am - 6pm.
(Last tour 4pm.)

November - February   Monday - Friday   9am - 5.30pm.
(Last tour 4pm.)

Potential saving - £2.50.

Based on 1996 adult admission price. (Note: 1997 savings may be even greater as many 1997 prices were not available at time of printing.)

Dunluce Centre

10 Sandhill Drive
Portrush
Co Antrim

Tel: (01265) 824444

Present this voucher when you purchase an *inclusive* ticket and receive another free of charge.

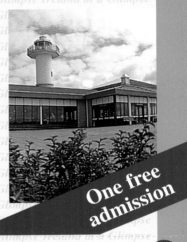

One free admission

Valid until 31 Dec 1997

Dunluce Castle

Dunluce
Co Antrim

Tel: (012657) 31938

Present this voucher and receive one free admission when a second of equal or greater value is purchased.

ENVIRONMENT
AND HERITAGE
SERVICE

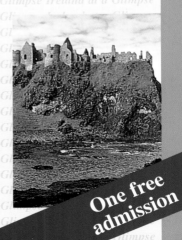

One free admission

Valid until 31 Dec 1997

Dunluce Centre

Fun, excitement and education for young and old alike.

- Turbo Tours; hi-tec action adventure, motion simulation at its best.

- Myths and legends; powerful special effects bring the history of the north coast to life before your very eyes.

- Earthquest; endless family fun in this interactive world of adventure.

- Viewing Tower; enjoy the spectacular views from a 45 foot high advantage.

Opening times:

To check opening hours before visiting phone (01265) 824444.

Potential saving - £4.50.

Based on 1996 adult or child admission price. (Note: 1997 savings may be even greater as many 1997 prices were not available at time of printing.)

Dunluce Castle

Dunluce is the largest and most sophisticated castle of the Northern Irish coastline. During the 16th Century it was home to the MacQuillans, and later the MacDonnells. A visit to this amazing place will remain in your memory for a long time.

Opening times:

1 April - 30 September.
Monday - Saturday:	10am - 7pm.
Sunday:	11am - 7pm.

1 October - 31 March.
Monday - Saturday	10am - 4pm.
Sunday:	2pm - 4pm.

Potential saving - £1.50.

Based on 1996 adult admission price. (Note: 1997 savings may be even greater as many 1997 prices were not available at time of printing.)

Giant's Causeway Centre

44 Causeway Road
Bushmills
Co Antrim

Tel: (012657) 31855

Present this voucher and receive one free admission to the Causeway Audio-Visual Presentation when a second of equal or greater value is purchased.

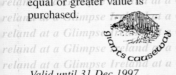

One free admission

Valid until 31 Dec 1997

Arthur Cottage

Dreen
Cullybackey
Co Antrim

Tel: (01266) 880781

Cordially invite you to one free admission when a second of equal or greater value is purchased.

ARTHUR COTTAGE
DREEN, CULLYBACKEY, NORTHERN IRELAND

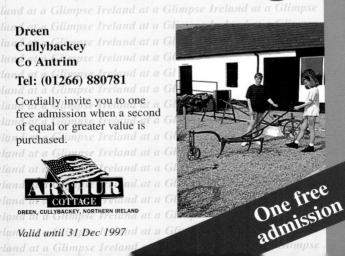

One free admission

Valid until 31 Dec 1997

Giant's Causeway Centre

At Northern Ireland's top tourist attraction, the award winning Giant's Causeway Visitor Centre incorporates an exhibition and an audio-visual presentation telling tales of GIANTS and GEOLOGY and highlights the many attractions of the Causeway Coast Area. The 25 minute presentation explores the origins of the 38,000 hexagonal shaped basalt columns which make up the 55 million year old causeway and introduces the visitor to the legendary Causeway Giant Finn McCool who is reputed to have created the Causeway to get across to Scotland.

Opening times:

January - March	Daily	10am - 4pm.
April - May	Daily	10am - 5pm.
June & September	Daily	10am - 6pm.
July & August	Daily	10am - 7pm.

Potential saving - £1.00.

Based on 1996 adult admission price. (Note: 1997 savings may be even greater as many 1997 prices were not available at time of printing.)

Arthur Cottage

The cottage situated Northwest of the village of Cullybackey is where the forebearers of Chester Alan Arthur, 21st President of the USA, once lived. An Interpretative Centre which sits alongside the cottage features displays of rural life in days gone by and the story of Arthur's Presidency. Craft demonstrations are held in June, July and August. Souvenirs, snack facilities and picnic tables are available.

Opening times:

1 May – 30 September:	Mon – Fri:	10.30am - 5pm.
	Sat:	10.30am - 4pm.

Potential saving - £1.00.

Based on 1996 adult admission price. (Note: 1997 savings may be even greater as many 1997 prices were not available at time of printing.)

Carrickfergus Castle

Carrickfergus
Co Antrim
Tel: (01960) 351273

Present this voucher and receive
one free admission when a
second of equal or greater value
is purchased.

**ENVIRONMENT
AND HERITAGE
SERVICE**

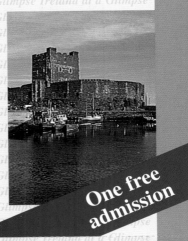

*One free
admission*

Valid until 31 Dec 1997

Knight Ride Heritage Plaza

Carrickfergus
Co Antrim
Tel: (01960) 366455

Cordially invite you to one
free admission when a second
of equal or greater value is
purchased.

*One free
admission*

Valid until 31 Dec 1997

Carrickfergus Castle

Carrickfergus Castle is one of the best preserved Norman castles in Ireland. It has recently undergone a significant enhancement programme and now has a video theatre, activity room, banquet display and exciting outdoor models depicting the turbulent history of the castle.

Opening times:

1 April – 30 September.

Monday – Saturday:	10am - 6pm.
Sunday:	2pm - 6pm.

1 October – 31 March.

Monday – Saturday:	10am - 4pm.
Sunday:	2pm - 4pm.

Potential saving - £2.70.

Based on 1996 adult admission price. (Note: 1997 savings may be even greater as many 1997 prices were not available at time of printing.)

Knight Ride Heritage Plaza

'Knight Ride' is the only monorail themed ride in Ireland. Step aboard one of the Ride's specially designed cars and experience over 1,000 years of Carrickfergus' exciting history. From the legendary shipwreck in 581 of the nobleman, Fergus – on the rock which gives the town its name – to the 19th Century market scene, you will see, hear and even smell the past of Ulster's liveliest town.

Opening times:

April - May:	Mon - Sat	10am - 6pm.
	Sun	12 noon - 6pm.
June - August:	Mon - Sat	10am - 6pm.
	Sun	12 noon - 6pm.
Sept:	Mon - Sat	10am - 6pm.
	Sun	12 noon - 6pm.
Oct - March:	Mon - Sat	10am - 5pm.
	Sun	12 noon - 5pm.

Potential saving - £2.70.

Based on 1996 adult admission price. (Note: 1997 savings may be even greater as many 1997 prices were not available at time of printing.)

Andrew Jackson Centre/
U.S. Ranger Exhibition

Boneybefore
Carrickfergus
Co Antrim

Tel: (01960) 366455

Cordially invite you to one
free admission when a second
of equal or greater value is
purchased.

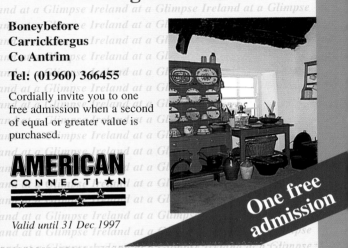

AMERICAN
C O N N E C T I ★ N

Valid until 31 Dec 1997

One free admission

Patterson's Spade Mill

Antrim Road
Templepatrick
Co Antrim

Tel: (01849) 433619

Cordially invites you and your
guest to enjoy one complimentary
ADMISSION when a second
ADMISSION of equal or greater
value is purchased.

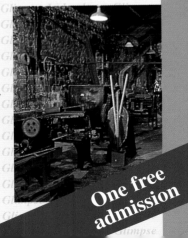

🍂 The National Trust

Valid until 31 Dec 1997,
during published opening times.
Not valid for special events.

One free admission

Andrew Jackson Centre/
U.S. Ranger Exhibition

Located in an Eighteenth Century thatched cottage, the Andrew Jackson Centre traces the Ulster-Scots Emigration to America and highlights the life and career of Andrew Jackson, 7th president of the United States of America. Also in the grounds of the Andrew Jackson Centre is the US Ranger exhibition, which is dedicated to the American soldiers who formed the First Ranger units in Carrickfergus during World War II.

Opening times:

Summer opening hours, Mon – Fri: 10am - 1pm
                                               2pm - 6pm.
                      Sat & Sun: 2pm - 6pm.

Potential saving - £1.20.

Based on 1996 adult admission price. (Note: 1997 savings may be even greater as many 1997 prices were not available at time of printing.)

Patterson's Spade Mill

The last surviving water-driven spade mill in Ireland. Spades were made here until 1990 and all the original equipment has been fully restored. There are demonstrations of spade making during normal opening times.

Opening times:

April, May and Sept: Sat, Sun and Bank Holidays:
                      2pm - 6pm.

June – August: Daily except Tues: 2pm - 6pm.

Potential saving - £2.50.

Based on 1996 adult admission price. (Note: 1997 savings may be even greater as many 1997 prices were not available at time of printing.)

Irish Linen Centre/ Lisburn Museum

Market Square
Lisburn
Co Antrim

Tel: (01846) 663377

Present this voucher
and receive one
free admission
when a second
of equal or
greater value
is purchased.

IRISH
LINEN
CENTRE

LISBURN
MUSEUM

Valid until 31 Dec 1997

One free admission

Lagan Lookout

Donegall Quay
Belfast

Tel: (01232) 315444

Present this voucher and
receive one free admission
when a second of equal or
greater value is purchased.

LAGAN LOOKOUT
VISITOR CENTRE

Valid until 31 Dec 1997

One free admission

Irish Linen Centre/
Lisburn Museum

Irish Museum of the year 1995.

The Irish Linen Centre tells the story of the Irish Linen industry from its origins to the present day. Visit the 'Factory Floor' of a 19th Century linen mill and chat with the weavers in the hand loom weaving workshop. You can also try your hand at many of the traditional processes involved in linen manufacture and afterwards relax in the speciality linen shop and coffee shop.

Opening times:

April – September:	Mon - Sat:	9.30am - 5.30pm.
	Sun:	2pm - 5.30pm.
October – March:	Mon - Sat:	9.30am - 5pm.
	Sun:	CLOSED.
Visit duration:	1 to 1½ hours.	
Last admission:	One hour before closing.	

Potential saving - £2.75.

Based on 1996 adult admission price. (Note: 1997 savings may be even greater as many 1997 prices were not available at time of printing.)

Lagan Lookout

Over the last three years the blue glow of the Lagan Weir has caught the eye of all who pass by. The Weir has signalled the return of the good times to the banks of Belfast's River Lagan and now the Lagan Lookout Visitors Centre located at the Donegall Quay side of the Weir allows the visitor to learn more about the Weir and Lagan's history.

The visitor to the Lagan Lookout can see how the Weir operates, hear the Harbour Masters tales of the old Port of Belfast.

Opening times:

March - September	Mon - Fri	11am - 5pm.
	Saturday	12 noon - 5pm.
	Sunday	2pm - 5pm.
October - February	Mon - Fri	11am - 3pm.
	Saturday	1pm - 4pm.
	Sunday	2pm - 4pm.

Potential saving - £1.50.

Based on 1996 adult admission price. (Note: 1997 savings may be even greater as many 1997 prices were not available at time of printing.)

Belfast Zoo

Antrim Road,
Belfast

Tel: (01232) 776277

This voucher entitles free
admission for one child *only*
when accompanied by a full
paying adult.

Valid until 31 Dec 1997

One free child admission

Citybus Tours

Tel: (01232) 458484

Present this voucher and
receive one free ticket when
an adult ticket is purchased for
the **MONDAY** afternoon tour.

Citybus Tours

Valid until 31 Dec 1997

One free admission

Belfast Zoo

Your visit to Belfast Zoo will take you through beautiful landscaped parkland with spectacular views over Belfast Lough and beyond. Enjoy the Children's Farm, Spider Monkey Island, the Primate Enclosure, African Enclosure, Penguin and Sea Lion Pools, Polar Bear Canyon, the newly-opened Bird Park, and much more.

Facilities include: Ark Restaurant, Snack Shop, Souvenir Shop, Picnic Tables and Free Parking.

Opening times:

April – September: 10am - 5pm.

October – March: 10am - 3.30pm (2.30pm on Fridays).

Open every day.

Potential saving - £2.10.

Based on 1996 child admission price. (Note: 1997 savings may be even greater as many 1997 prices were not available at time of printing.)

Citybus Tours

Enjoy a Monday afternoon in and around Greater Belfast with Citybus Tours. Our Monday afternoon tour programme varies throughout the summer offering something for everyone. From the historic buildings in Belfast City Centre to the attractions and scenery of the coastline to the south east of Belfast and its surrounding area. Further information is available from Citybus Tours on (01232) 458484.

Operating times:

June, July & August Every Monday departing at 1.30pm.

Potential saving - £7.00.

Based on 1996 adult admission price. (Note: 1997 savings may be even greater as many 1997 prices were not available at time of printing.)

The Brontë Homeland Interpretative Centre

**Church Hill, Rathfriland
Co Down**

Tel: (018206) 31152

Present this voucher and
receive one free admission
when a second of equal or
greater value is purchased.

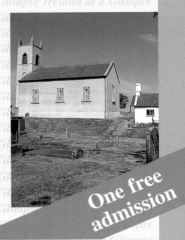

BANBRIDGE
DISTRICT COUNCIL

Valid until 31 Dec 1997

One free admission

Ulster Folk and Transport Museum

94

**Cultra, Holywood,
Co Down**

Tel: (01232) 428428

Present this voucher and we
will allow you one free
admission when a second of
equal or greater value is
purchased.

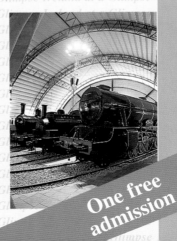

Valid until 31 Dec 1997

One free admission

The Brontë Homeland Interpretative Centre

The name Brontë or Brunty, in various forms, has been associated with this delightful part of Northern Ireland for over two hundred years. The area of County Down which is now known as the Brontë Country lies to the south of Banbridge.

The fertile land of County Down has been farming country for centuries. It was here that Patrick Brontë, father of Charlotte, Emily and Anne - the famous Brontë sisters, was born into a farming family on 17 March 1777 - St Patrick's Day!

Opening times:

March - October	Tues - Fri	11am - 5pm.
	Sat & Sun	2pm - 6pm.

Potential saving - £1.00.

based on 1996 Adult admission price. (Note: 1997 savings may be even greater as many 1997 prices were not available at time of printing.)

Ulster Folk and Transport Museum

Open Air Museum of: reconstructed farms, with their own farm animals; cottages; watermills; a small town with shops, a school, churches, printer's workshop, bank and terraces, all of which recreate the Ulster landscape of the 1900s.

Indoor Museum of popular culture, changing ways of life and transport through the ages. Major new attractions are the award-winning Irish Railway Collection and Road Transport Galleries.

Opening times:

Open all year round! (Closed three days during the Christmas period only.) Telephone (01232) 428428 or our 24-hour information line on 421444 for details of opening times.

Potential saving - £3.60.

Based on 1996 adult admission price. (Note: 1997 savings may be even greater as many 1997 prices were not available at time of printing.)

Mount Stewart

Newtownards
Co Down
Tel: (01247) 88387

Cordially invites you and your
guest to enjoy one complimentary
ADMISSION when a second
ADMISSION of equal or greater
value is purchased.

 The National Trust

Valid until 31 Dec 1997,
during published opening times.
Not valid for special events.

One free admission

Somme Heritage Centre

233 Bangor Road
Newtownards
Co Down
Tel: (01247) 823202

Present this voucher and
receive one free admission
when a second of equal or
greater value is purchased.

Valid until 31 Dec 1997

One free admission

Mount Stewart

Fascinating Eighteenth Century house with Nineteenth Century additions, home of Lord Castlereagh; one of the greatest gardens in these islands, largely created by the wife of the seventh Marquis of Londonderry, with an unrivalled collection of rare and unusual plants, colourful parterres and magnificent formal and informal vista. The Temple of the Winds, James 'Athenian' Stuart's banqueting hall of 1785, overlooks Strangford Lough.

Opening times:

House:	April and Oct: weekends only	1pm - 6pm.
	Easter (March 28th - April 6th) Daily	1pm - 6pm.
	May - September (including Bank Holidays)	
	Daily (except Tues)	1pm - 6pm.
Garden:	Open Sundays during March	2pm - 5pm.
	April to end Sept Daily	10.30am - 6pm.
	Weekends only	10.30am - 6pm.

Potential saving - £3.00.

Based on 1996 adult admission price to the house, gardens and Temple of the Winds. (Note: 1997 savings may be even greater as many 1997 prices were not available at time of printing.)

Somme Heritage Centre

The Somme Heritage Centre commemorates Ireland's involvement in the First World War, and enables visitors to travel back in time to the trenches of the First World War. Features include staff members dressed in period military dress, audio-visual displays and a reconstructed front-line trench to recreate the Battle of the Somme in 1916. Coffee and gift shop with ample parking.

Opening times (last tour one hour before closing):

October - March	Monday - Thursday	10am - 4pm
	Saturday	12 noon - 4pm
April, May & Sept	Monday - Thursday	10am - 4pm
	Saturday & Sunday	12 noon - 4pm
July & August	Monday - Friday	10am - 5pm
	Saturday & Sunday	12 noon - 5pm

Potential saving - £3.50.

Based on 1996 adult admission price. (Note: 1997 savings may be even greater as many 1997 prices were not available at time of printing.)

Castle Espie - Wildfowl & Wetlands Trust

Ballydrain Road
Comber
Co Down

Tel: (01247) 874146

Present this voucher and
receive one free admission
when a second of equal or
greater value is purchased.

THE
WILDFOWL
& WETLANDS TRUST

Valid until 31 Dec 1997

One free admission

Grey Abbey

Greyabbey
Co Down

Tel: (01247) 788585

Present this voucher and
receive one free admission
when a second of equal or
greater value is purchased.

ENVIRONMENT
AND HERITAGE
SERVICE

Valid until 31 Dec 1997

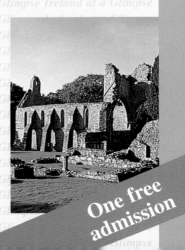

One free admission

Castle Espie - Wildfowl & Wetlands Trust

Castle Espie holds the largest collection of wildfowl in Ireland in a wonderful setting on the shores of Strangford Lough. Many rare and exotic birds will feed from your hand, and from woodland walks and bird hides, thousands of wild birds can also be seen. There is also an excellent restaurant, art gallery and gift shop overlooking beautifully landscaped waterfowl gardens.

Opening times:

November – February.
Monday – Saturday: 11.30am - 4pm.
Sunday   11.30am - 5pm.

March – October.
Monday – Saturday: 10.30am - 5pm.
Sunday   11.30am - 6pm.
Closed Christmas Day.

Potential saving - £2.75.

Based on 1996 adult admission price. (Note: 1997 savings may be even greater as many 1997 prices were not available at time of printing.)

Grey Abbey

Situated in beautiful parkland, the Abbey, founded in 1193 by Affreca, wife of John de Courcey, is a pleasure to visit. A medieval herb garden, with over 50 varieties and a visitors' centre are the recent additions to the attraction.

Opening times:

1 April – 30 September.

Tuesday – Saturday: 10am - 7pm.

Sunday: 2pm - 7pm.

Potential saving - £1.00.

Based on 1996 adult admission price. (Note: 1997 savings may be even greater as many 1997 prices were not available at time of printing.)

Exploris

**Castle Street
Portaferry
Co Down**

Tel: (012477) 28062

Present this voucher and receive one free admission when a second of equal or greater value is purchased.

AN EXPLORATION OF THE IRISH SEA

Valid until 31 Dec 1997

One free admission

Streamvale Farm

**38 Ballyhanwood Road
Belfast**

Tel: (01232) 483244

Cordially invite you to a free admission when a second of equal or greater value is purchased.

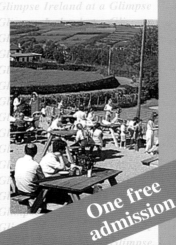

Valid until 31 Dec 1997

One free admission

Exploris

Hundreds of species from the marine life of the Irish Sea, in one of Europe's finest marine displays. Stroke the animals in the Touch Tank, watch majestic rays and circling sharks in the huge Open Sea tank (one of the largest in the UK), and be surrounded by hundreds of gleaming fish in the Shoaling Ring.

Opening times:

April - September:	Monday - Friday	10am - 6pm.
	Saturday	11am - 6pm.
	Sunday	1pm - 6pm.
October-March:	Monday - Friday	10am - 5pm.
	Saturday	11am - 5pm.
	Sunday	1pm - 5pm.

Potential saving - £3.50.

Based on 1996 adult admission price. (Note: 1997 savings may be even greater as many 1997 prices were not available at time of printing.)

Streamvale Farm

Streamvale is a family-run dairy farm set in the Gilnahirk hills, overlooking Belfast. Come along to watch the milking and feed the animals. Enjoy the full range of farm and pet animals in the Pets Corner. We have a Straw Bounce, Nature Trail, Outdoor Play Area, Picnic Area and Tea room. Get involved! Hand milk a goat, cuddle a fluffy chick, have a tractor & trailor ride, watch the sheep racing.

Opening times:

Feb - May	Wed, Sat & Sun	2pm - 6pm.
June	Every day	12pm - 6pm.
July and Aug	Every day	10.30am - 6pm.
Sept - Oct	Wed, Sat & Sun	2pm - 6pm.
Also Easter week and May Day		10.30am - 6pm.

Potential saving - £2.50.

Based on 1996 adult admission price. (Note: 1997 savings may be even greater as many 1997 prices were not available at time of printing.)

Rowallane

Saintfield
Co Down

Tel: (01238) 510131

Cordially invites you and your guest to enjoy one complimentary ADMISSION when a second ADMISSION of equal or greater value is purchased.

 The National Trust

Valid until 31 Dec 1997, during published opening times. Not valid for special events.

One free admission

Castle Ward

Strangford
Co Down

Tel: (01396) 881204

Cordially invites you and your guest to enjoy one complimentary ADMISSION when a second ADMISSION of equal or greater value is purchased.

 The National Trust

Valid until 31 Dec 1997, during published opening times. Not valid for special events.

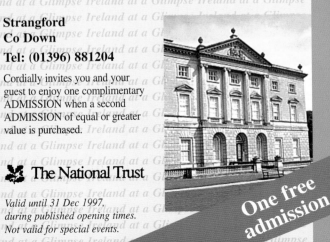

One free admission

Rowallane

52 acres of natural garden with plants from many parts of the world. Daffodils and rhododendrons in spring reach their peak around the end of May to early June; summer flowering trees and shrubs continue the display; in the Wall Garden herbaceous plants, including the National Collection of Penstemon along with fuchsias and shrub roses will flower until autumn frost; the rock garden is interesting throughout the year. Autumn brings a spectacular display of foliage and berries.

Opening times:

1 April - end Oct	Mon - Fri	10.30am - 6pm.
	Sat and Sun	2pm - 6pm.
Nov to end March 1997	Mon - Fri	10.30 am - 5pm.

Potential saving - £2.50.

Based on 1996 adult admission price. (Note: 1997 savings may be even greater as many 1997 prices were not available at time of printing.)

Castle Ward

700-acre country estate with woodland, lake and seashore; unique eighteenth century house with facades in different styles; the west front Classical, the east front Gothic; Victorian laundry; formal and landscaped gardens with fine shrubs and specimen trees; fortified tower house and saw mill; wildfowl collection; information centre, restaurant and shop; theatre in stable yard. Restored Cornmill with exhibition.

Opening times:

House: April, Sept and Oct	Sat and Sun	1pm - 6pm.
Easter (March 28th - April 6th)		
	Daily	1pm - 6pm.
May – August	Daily (except Thurs)	1pm - 6pm.

Estate and Grounds: Open all year dawn to dusk.

Potential saving - £2.60.

Based on 1996 adult admission price. (Note: 1997 savings may be even greater as many 1997 prices were not available at time of printing.)

The Navan Centre

81 Killylea Road
Armagh
Co Armagh
Tel: (01861) 525550

Cordially invite you to one free admission when a second of equal or greater value is purchased.

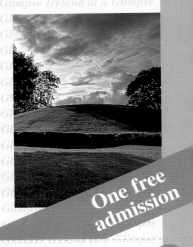

NAVAN
ANCIENT CAPITAL OF ULSTER

Valid until 31 Dec 1997

One free admission

St Patrick's Trian

English Street
Armagh
Co Armagh
Tel: (01861) 521801

Cordially invite you to one free admission when a second of equal or greater value is purchased. Not valid for groups, special or educational visits.

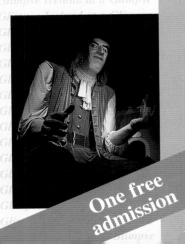

SAINT PATRICK'S TRIAN
ARMAGH

Valid until 31 Dec 1997

One free admission

The Navan Centre

Navan Fort is one of Europe's most important Celtic sites; seat of the ancient Kings of Ulster and setting for the legends of the mythical CuChulainn. The Navan Centre unravels the history and archaeology of Navan Fort in an award-winning exhibition.

Opening times:

July – August:	Mon – Sat	10.00am - 7.00pm.
	Sun	11.00am - 7.00pm.
April – June & Sept	Mon – Sat	10.00am - 6.00pm.
	Sun	11.00am - 6.00pm.
Oct – March	Mon – Fri	10.00am - 5.00pm.
	Sat	11.00am - 5.00pm.
	Sun	12.00am - 5.00pm.

Potential saving - £3.95.

Based on 1996 adult admission price. (Note: 1997 savings may be even greater as many 1997 prices were not available at time of printing.)

St Patrick's Trian

New interpretive centre which illustrates 'The Armagh Story' – the development of Armagh from prehistoric times to the present. Also, 'the Land of Lilliput' is a child-centred fantasy based on 'Gulliver's Travels'. Other features include St Patrick exhibition, craft workshops, educational facilities and Pilgrim's Table restaurant.

Opening times:

April - September:	Mon - Sat	10am - 5.30pm.
	Sun	1pm - 6pm.
Oct - March:	Mon - Sat	10am - 5pm.
	Sun	2pm - 5pm.

Potential saving - £3.25.

Based on 1996 adult admission price. (Note: 1997 savings may be even greater as many 1997 prices were not available at time of printing.)

Palace Stables

The Palace Demesne
Armagh, Co Armagh
Tel: (01861) 529629

Cordially invite you to one free admission when a second of equal or greater value is purchased. Not valid for groups, special or educational visits.

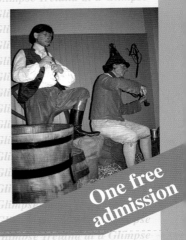

Valid until 31 Dec 1997

One free admission

Ardress House

Annaghamore
Co Armagh
Tel: (01762) 851236

Cordially invites you and your guest to enjoy one complimentary ADMISSION when a second ADMISSION of equal or greater value is purchased.

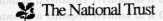 **The National Trust**

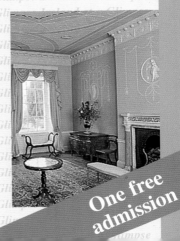

Valid until 31 Dec 1997,
during published opening times.
Not valid for special events.

One free admission

Palace Stables

Interpretive centre housed in a Georgian stable block, adjacent to the former Archbishop of the Church of Ireland residence. Guided tours conducted to 'A Day in the Life' exhibition, Primates Chapel, servants tunnel and ice house. Also horse-drawn carriage rides, Stables restaurant, picnic area and ecotrail.

Opening times:

April – September:	Mon – Sat	10am - 5.30pm.
	Sun	1pm - 6pm.
Oct – March	Mon – Sat	10am - 5pm.
	Sun	2pm - 5pm.

Potential saving - £2.80.

Based on 1996 adult admission price. (Note: 1997 savings may be even greater as many 1997 prices were not available at time of printing.)

Ardress House

Seventeenth Century farmhouse, main front and garden facades added in Eighteenth Century by owner architect George Ensor; neoclassical plasterwork in drawing room; good furniture and pictures; display of farm implements and livestock in farmyard; garden; woodland walks; playground.

Opening times:

April, May and Sept; Sat, Sun and Bank Holidays:		2pm - 6pm.
Easter (March 28th - April 1st)	Daily	2pm - 6pm.
June – August	Daily (except Tues)	2pm - 6pm.
Farmyard also open May and Sept; weekdays except Tues:		12pm - 4pm.

Potential saving - £2.10.

Based on 1996 adult admission price. (Note: 1997 savings may be even greater as many 1997 prices were not available at time of printing.)

Lough Neagh Discovery Centre

Oxford Island National Nature Reserve Craigavon

Tel: (01762) 322205

Cordially invite you to one free admission when a second of equal or greater value is purchased.

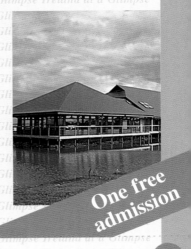

Valid until 31 Dec 1997

One free admission

County Museum

The Carroll Centre Jocelyn Street Dundalk Co Louth

Tel: (042) 27056

Present this voucher and receive one free admission when a second of equal or greater value is purchased.

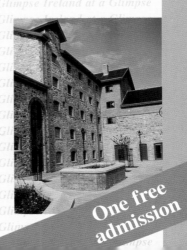

Valid until 31 Dec 1997

One free admission

Lough Neagh Discovery Centre

The Lough Neagh Discovery Centre is recognised as one of Northern Ireland's most innovative visitor attractions, telling the story of the Lough's wildlife, history and management, by its two audio-visual shows, touchscreen computer room and interactive displays. Situated in Oxford Island, Craigavon, it also has a cafe and gift shop, plus bird-watching hides and miles of footpaths through the reserve's habitats.

Opening times:

April – September: 10am - 7pm every day.

October – March: 10am - 5pm Wednesday – Sunday.
                    Closed Monday and Tuesday.

Potential saving - £2.80.

Based on 1996 adult admission price. (Note: 1997 savings may be even greater as many 1997 prices were not available at time of printing.)

County Museum

The County Museum is housed in a beautifully restored late 18th century warehouse and offers four floors of excellent exhibition space. The ground floor display is on the history of industry in County Louth. The remaining floors contain temporary exhibitions on a wide variety of subjects. The 72 seater film theatre shows a 13 minute presentation on the history and development of County Louth. Group activities for children such as painting, clay modelling, quizzes, etc are provided for in the specially fitted activities room. All floors have disabled access. Car parking is available to the rear of the building and coffee shops are adjacent to the building.

Opening times:

May – Sept	Monday – Saturday	10.30am - 5.30pm.
	Sunday & Bank Holidays	2pm - 6pm.
Oct – April	Tuesday – Saturday	10.30am - 5.30pm.
	Sunday & Bank Holidays	2pm - 6pm.

Potential saving - £2.00.

Based on 1996 adult admission price. (Note: 1997 savings may be even greater as many 1997 prices were not available at time of printing.)

Northern Ireland's
Heartland

Step across our threshold in to the undiscovered country called Welcome.

Located in the heart of Northern Ireland overlooking County Antrim's rich dairy lands, with Lough Neagh just minutes away and within easy reach of many wonderful tourist attractions, the Aldergrove Hotel offers a modern cosmopolitan base for your holiday.

Finished to the highest standards, sound proofed and fully air conditioned throughout we have everything you would expect from a leading hotel not forgetting good old down to earth hospitality...

... so indulge yourself in our country of Welcome.

THE ALDERGROVE
AIRPORT HOTEL
"In the Heart of Northern Ireland"

Belfast International Airport Belfast BT29 4AB N. Ireland
Telephone 44 1849 422033 Facsimile 44 1849 423500

Clue

You've arrived at a
Victorian Palm House,
it's not in London.

Where could you be?

Solution **Belfast**

Take it all in.

A cruise on the Fermanagh Lakes. A hill walk in the Sperrins. Breathe in the beauty of the Giant's Causeway. The Mountains of Mourne. The green Glens of Antrim.

Touch the history of Derry. Of Armagh's Cathedral city. And the warmth of the people.

Golf. Fishing. Sailing. Horse-riding. Activities awaiting discovery in idyllic surroundings. Superb restaurants. Pubs and live entertainment. You're really spoilt for choice.

And don't forget to visit Belfast. A city steeped in history with a fine tradition of culture, crafts, sports and business.

Mussenden Temple, Downhill

Belfast	St. Anne's Court, 59 North Street, Belfast BT11NB Tel: (01232) 246609
Dublin	16 Nassau Street, Dublin 2 Tel: (003531) 6791977
London	11 Berkeley Street, London W1X 5AD Tel: (0171) 355 5040
Glasgow	135 Buchanan Street, 1st Floor, Glasgow G1 2JA Tel: (0141) 204 4454
France	3 Rue de Pontoise, 78100 St. Germain-en-Laye Tel: (00331) 39 21 93 80
Germany	Taunusstr 52 60, 60329 Frankfurt/Main Tel: (004969) 234 504
USA	551 Fifth Avenue, Suite 701, New York, NY 10176 Tel: (001212) 922 0101
Canada	111 Avenue Rd, Suite 450, Toronto, Ontario M5R Tel: (001416) 925 6368

Northern Ireland
Tourist Board